THE SALVATION OF DOCTOR WHO

MATT RAWLE

THE SALVATION OF
DOCTOR WHO

A SMALL GROUP STUDY
CONNECTING CHRIST AND CULTURE

Abingdon Press / Nashville

THE SALVATION OF DOCTOR WHO
A SMALL GROUP STUDY
CONNECTING CHRIST AND CULTURE

This book is printed on elemental, chlorine-free paper.
ISBN 978-1-5018-0380-2

15 16 17 18 19 20 21 22 23 24—10 9 8 7 6 5 4 3 2 1
MANUFACTURED IN THE UNITED STATES OF AMERICA

To Marlene and Rick Rawle

CONTENTS

INTRODUCTION

What comes to mind when you hear someone refer to pop culture?

Maybe you think about the newest playlist on Spotify or the new releases on Netflix or the top-grossing smartphone apps. Or maybe you think of something more under the radar. Sometimes pop culture begins with a small, fanatic fan base who loves a relatively unknown book, movie, band, or artist. Maybe there's the band you never hear on the radio but everyone's talking about. Or that series of novels you think looks weird but that inspires legions of people to write "fan fiction" surrounding its main characters. Sometimes, instead of becoming trendy, these artists retain a faithful, insider following. They become less "pop" and more "cult," becoming what is known as a "cult classic."

Regardless if you picture an example of "pop culture" as an innovative hit like *Breaking Bad* or something more fanatic and underground like *Firefly*, there's no denying that the popular music, books, television, movies, and media have much to say about the world in which we live. The word *culture* is used often, by many different people in many different ways, but in its simplest form, *culture* is simply an expression of how a community understands itself. God, our Creator, supplies us with the raw ingredients of humanity—talents, time, creativity, desires, ingenuity—and "culture" is whatever we cook up. Stories, songs, recipes, traditions, art, and language are all displays of how we interpret the world and our place in it.

So what role does God play in our culture—in our day-to-day lives and in the work of our hands, which produces music and art and literature and plays and movies and technology? Throughout history, people have debated this issue and adamantly drawn a dividing line between that which should be considered "sacred" (that which is explicitly religious in nature) and that which should be considered "secular" (that is, everything else). At first glance, these may be seemingly easy judgments to make, but when we stop to examine what God has to say about this division, we might be surprised at what we find.

Scripture says that *all* things were made through Christ (John 1:3), and through Christ *all* things were reconciled to God (Colossians 1:20). In other words, everything and everyone in our world contains a spark of the divine—everything is sacred, and whether or not we choose to live in that truth depends on our perspective. For example, think of sunlight as a holy (sacred) gift from God. God offers us sunlight so that we can see the world around us. We can celebrate the sacred by creating things that enhance the light in our homes, such as larger windows or skylights, or we can hang heavy drapes and close the shutters in order to diminish the sacred and shut out the light. Our sacred work is letting in as much light as possible, and those things that keep the light out need to be rejected or transformed.

Through Jesus, God put on flesh and walked among us, in our

world, in order to re-narrate what it means to be a child of God. God assumed culture and transformed it. So now all is sacred, and in everything we are to see and proclaim his glory. I truly believe we are called not to reject the culture we live in, but to re-narrate its meaning—to tell God's story in the midst of it. Jesus didn't reject the cross (the sin of our world); rather, Jesus accepted it and transformed it from a death instrument into a symbol of life and reconciliation.

The Pop in Culture

Sometimes it's easy to see God in the midst of culture—in the stories of Scripture and in reverent hymns and worshipful icons. Other times the divine is more veiled—hidden in a novel, concealed in classic rock, obscured by an impressionist's palate.

As we walk with Christ, we discover the divine all around us, and in turn, the world invites us into a deeper picture of its Creator. Through this lens of God's redemption story, we are invited to look at culture in a new and inviting way. We are invited to dive into the realms of literature, art, and entertainment to explore and discover how God is working in and through us and in the world around us to tell his great story of redemption.

The Pop in Culture series is a collection of studies about faith and popular culture. Each study uses a work of pop culture as a way to examine questions and issues of the Christian faith. Studies consist of a book, DVD, and leader guide. Our hope and prayer is that the studies will open our eyes to the spiritual truths that exist all around us in books, movies, music, and television.

The Salvation of Doctor Who

How we understand identity, our connection with time, and the importance of salvation are all themes in the popular British television program *Doctor Who*. First airing in 1963, *Doctor Who* is one of the longest running and most influential shows in the history of television. Over the last fifty years, the audience has traveled with the main character—known only as the Doctor—across all of time and space as he fights in the battle between good and evil.

Begun as a children's program meant to teach history, *Doctor Who* has evolved into an age-spanning favorite. The Doctor has become a cultural icon who represents the power of good over evil. Seen through eyes of faith, *Doctor Who* can be a lens through which we understand who we are and our connection with God's saving grace.

In this study, we will explore four ways that *Doctor Who* can prompt us to ask deep theological questions, and why these questions matter. We begin with asking the seemingly oldest question in the universe: "Who am I?" We'll ask the question, "When we talk about our identity, what exactly are we talking about?" Next we will think about how God interacts with time, how we can connect with a God who is timeless, and how that affects our understanding of salvation. Then we will dive into many of the great villains in *Doctor Who* and discover what they reveal about the nature of sin and redemption. Finally, we will consider just how deep God's love for us is, and how we can learn to live in that love. Each chapter is divided into five sections, perfect for daily readings, with questions for reflection at the end of each section.

Sometimes it can be hard to ask difficult questions of our faith, to risk deep answers to hard questions. Having questions about faith doesn't mean that our faith is not where it needs to be, or that we dishonor tradition or authority. I believe that when we open the doors of our churches and our communities to the hard questions of faith, God is delighted to come in and work in those places. Studying *Doctor Who* offers a fun and unexpected way to help us think about and talk about our faith in different and helpful ways. It also gives us an opportunity to share a Christ-centered experience with those who may have never experienced the love of a Christian community.

Doctor Who tells the story of the timelessness and power of goodness and truth in a universe that hate and sin have broken. The good news is that the Doctor, an image of Christ as the Great Physician (see Acts 10:38), reveals that there is always hope for those who fight for mercy, grace, and love. *Doctor Who* entertainingly stretches our minds about what is so that we might fully worship the God who created everything that is.

DOCTOR WHO

A QUICK REFRESHER

First airing in 1963, the popular British science-fiction television program *Doctor Who* is the story of a time-traveling alien, the Doctor, who tours all of time and space to fight for goodness against the forces of evil. The Doctor is a member of an alien race called the "Time Lords" from the planet Gallifrey. For millions of years the Time Lords have lived near a tear in the fabric of space time (called the Untempered Schism) and have developed the technology to travel through time and space using a vehicle called a TARDIS, an acronym meaning "Time and Relative Dimension in Space." The Doctor's TARDIS, which was created to blend in with its surroundings, wherever it lands, looks like an iconic blue English police box from the early 1960s. Because of a malfunctioning chameleon circuit (obviously), the TARDIS remains stuck in this form, no matter where it ends up. The TARDIS has a conscience all its own and takes the Doctor where he's most needed, even if it's not where he wants to go.

The Doctor lives to fight evil alien races bent on destroying the universe. The Daleks, Cybermen, Silence, Weeping Angels, and more have kept the Doctor busy for the last fifty years. Every now and again these villains will gain the upper hand and mortally wound the Doctor, but thankfully (especially if you produce *Doctor Who*), the Doctor can heal himself through a process called, "regeneration." When the Doctor regenerates, almost every cell in his body is made new, and therefore he looks like a different person each time it happens. Each of the Doctor's incarnations is different—sometimes the Doctor appears as an old, fatherly gentleman. Other times the Doctor seems to be a young, childlike hipster. It all depends on what kind of hero the producers—ahem, I mean, the *universe*—needs.

The Doctor is basically a superhero, and every great superhero needs a sidekick. One of the things that separates *Doctor Who* from other good-versus-evil stories is the importance of the sidekick, or in this case, the "companion." The companion—the Doctor's traveling buddy—is an integral part of *Doctor Who*. Without a companion, the Doctor quickly becomes bitter, vengeful, and short-tempered. It seems that his various companions offer a helpful accountability to the Doctor, who sometimes succumbs to his own ego and superior intellect. In a way, the audience is also like the Doctor's companion, or at least, the audience lives vicariously through the companion's adventures with the Doctor. Just like a television program needs an audience, the Doctor just isn't the same all by himself.

In addition to regeneration, the Doctor fights the power of evil with a superior intellect (he's about two thousand years old, so he's seen a few things), the ability to time travel (it's quite an advantage when you can go backward in time and fix your mistakes), and a sonic screwdriver (yep, it's literally a screwdriver that uses sound to manipulate its surroundings, though it doesn't work on wood, oddly enough). He doesn't carry a gun, he doesn't have super strength, and he usually avoids violence. In other words, he is the superhero all we geeks aspire to be. I can't beat Goliath using muscle, but if I understand physics well enough, a well-slung rock will do just fine.

Doctor Who is one of the most popular franchises in pop culture history because it is so much more than a simple story of good versus evil. The story is unique and almost hidden in plain sight. Like the TARDIS, it can be out in the open, completely missed, but hold the secrets of the vast universe inside. Likewise, loyal *Doctor Who* fans know that a bow tie is more than a bow tie, a scarf is more than a scarf, and a blue phone box represents, well, everything. Here we have a two-thousand-year-old hero who can move in and out of time and who always invites companions to join him on a journey to save all of creation from the power of evil. This all sounds strangely familiar....

Chapter One

THE OLDEST QUESTION IN THE UNIVERSE

Jesus and his disciples went into the villages near Caesarea Philippi. On the way he asked his disciples, "Who do people say that I am?" – Mark 8:27

One of the oldest questions in the universe is "Who am I?" In a way, this is the central question the universe asks of itself. You see, all of the heavy elements in our bodies were created deep within the heart of stars, millions of light years away from us. When those stars exploded, these elements traveled across the universe to the earth. It was the dust out of which God formed humanity. As my dad once told me, "You are very intentionally made. The God who hung the stars had to shake them in order for you to be." We are intimately connected to the universe that surrounds us.

"Who am I?" is the first place where Scripture and *Doctor Who* collide. In this chapter we will ponder how God's Word and the words of the Doctor help us understand the beauty of God's creation and our role within it.

One of the most interesting things about *Doctor Who* is that twelve different actors have portrayed the Time Lord from Gallifrey, and the audience buys the fact that all twelve actors are the same person. Why does the audience accept that twelve different personalities all share the same identity? It's not so hard to believe when you think about it. My guess is that if you ask twelve different people to describe you, you just might get twelve different answers. And are you who they think you are? Maybe; maybe not. Maybe you are simply a child of God and a follower of Christ, and that's all the world needs to know.

Fifty Years of Who

The BBC science fiction program *Doctor Who* first aired in November of 1963. Not only is *Doctor Who* record-setting as one of the longest running television programs (it would take you nearly four hundred hours to watch every episode) but its list of "firsts" was groundbreaking in the television industry. The theme song, written by Ron Grainer, realized by Delia Derbyshire, and celebrated by geeks everywhere, was one of the first electronically composed pieces of music. Verity Lambert, one of *Doctor Who's* founding producers, was the youngest and only female producer working for the BBC. And the Fourth Doctor, Tom Baker, still holds the record for the longest scarf ever worn on television.

Doctor Who has never shied away from innovation, offering the world timeless cultural icons—from the ordinary blue police box to the sublime but terrifying distorted "Exterminate!" scream of a Dalek. The creative team at the BBC is a master of subversive marketing and storytelling. For example, a bow tie is just a bow tie, unless you are a fan of *Doctor Who* and know that Matt Smith, the Eleventh Doctor, was never seen without it. In terms of culture, *Doctor Who* is like geek camouflage. The symbols, like bow ties and garden statues, are out in the open, but only insiders know their hidden meanings.

The show's countercultural expression began right from the beginning. As the audience comes to find out, the show's title—stemming from the question "Doctor Who?"—is the oldest and most important question in the universe, the answer hiding in plain sight.

WHO IS THE DOCTOR?

"Doctor who?" — Asked by many, nearly forty times over the show's fifty-year history

Who is the Doctor anyway? Perhaps a more intriguing question is "When?" or "Where?" is the Doctor. When you travel through all of time and space, as the Doctor does, your identity isn't so easy to pin down. Nevertheless, we do know that the Doctor is a Time Lord, one of a race of alien beings from the planet Gallifrey, who travels around the universe fighting bad guys and righting wrongs. His vehicle of choice is called the TARDIS, which stands for "Time and Relative Dimension in Space." Along with his sonic screwdriver and a companion or two, the Doctor travels anywhere and anytime in order to rid the universe of evil.

THAT'S A LOT OF TIME...

It would take 362 hours, 53 minutes, and 43 seconds to watch every episode of *Doctor Who.*

Over the last fifty years, the loyal audience of *Doctor Who*, one of the BBC's most popular programs, has grown quite familiar with what the Doctor does, but he is still a character who is hard to pin down. In the episode "Asylum of the Daleks,"[1] the Doctor comes face-to-face with perhaps his greatest enemy, the Daleks—a race of genetically altered beings created to exterminate every creature who isn't one of them. In a strange plot twist, the Daleks ask the Doctor to travel to the Dalek asylum and do away with the Daleks who have gone mad who now threaten the existence of the Dalek race. The Doctor questions why they wouldn't just do away with their own who don't measure up, and the Daleks reveal that it is against their culture to destroy such "divine hatred," which is why they have never been able to kill him. The Daleks call the Doctor "The Predator" because of how many of them he has killed. So, is the Doctor a terrorist or a freedom fighter? In this episode, he is both.

Identity can be a tricky thing to explain. For example, suppose I asked you the question: Who are you? If I asked you to write a three-sentence bio about yourself, what would you say? How do you describe your identity? Would you start with what you do or where you're from? Maybe you feel your accomplishments say the most about you. If I asked ten of your friends to describe you, what would they say? Would I get ten different answers? Who would be right?

Maybe the answer to the "Who am I?" is just your own version of the truth. Try this: close your eyes and say your name to yourself. What do you see? Do you see your face? Maybe you see your office or your family. Maybe you see a word like *honest* or *brave* or *failure* or *flawed*. But is this accurate of who you are?

Some would say that we are who we *think* we are; others would argue that we are what we say—that our words reveal who we really are deep down. There's a lot of truth in this understanding—after all, our legal system is, in large part, based on the power of words. At the end of a trial, the jury says, "We find the defendant *guilty* (or *not guilty*)," and these words have a dramatic effect on the identity of the person being judged. But the spoken word can be trusted only if the speaker is reliable. For example, "Follow me, and the world will be at peace," sounds like the gospel when Jesus says it, but means something else entirely from Lex Luthor.

Still others would say that we are what we do—for instance, a hammer is a hammer because it can successfully drive a nail. A hammer will never be a baseball no matter how well you throw it, right? A lot of us tend to think about identity in terms of what we can do. When you meet someone new, what is the first thing you ask? You probably ask them what they do. Culturally speaking, we tend to place a very high value on what one does, but can that theory be trusted? If I'm on the losing flag football team, does that make me a loser? If so, for how long? Until the next win? What if I stole a pencil from the grocery store when I was in the second grade? Does that make me a thief? If so, for how long? Until I bring the pencil back? Until I ask for forgiveness? What if I do something heroic? Am I a hero until I do something cowardly?

GREAT LENGTHS

The Fourth Doctor's iconic long scarf was created when the costume designer gave the knitter several balls of yarn to choose from to make the scarf, and instead, she knitted them all together.

So am I what I think? Or what I say? Am I what I do? Maybe all are true, but none of that takes into account what the gospel says about us. Jesus spent a great deal of time in John's Gospel teaching his disciples through several "I am," statements:

> "I am the light of the world." (John 8:12)
> "I am the bread of life." (John 6:35)
> "I am the way, the truth, and the life."(John 14:6)

Jesus' identity—his "I am"—finds its roots beyond thoughts, words, or actions. When Jesus says, "I am," he is pointing to who

God is. In other words, in order to discover a deeper understanding of who we are, we must look to our Creator. When our thoughts are directed toward love of God and love of neighbor, when our words reflect the word of God found in Scripture, when our actions mirror God's lifting up of the underdog, then we discover our true identity as a child of God.

At times our actions don't reflect God's love. Sometimes we fail to love our neighbor or even remember God in our daily to-dos. The good news is that God offers us forgiveness through Jesus' death and resurrection, so no matter what, our identity is rooted and grounded in the person of Jesus. Even when we make mistakes, our identity is restored through what Jesus has done for us. So identity is not what we think or say or do—it is what Christ has said and done for us.

In what ways has your identity changed over the last few years?

Do you consider yourself the same person you were five, ten, fifteen years ago? Why?

What is the basic identity of a Christian? Is it rooted in faith? Action? Grace?

HAVING TWO HEARTS

A good person produces good from the good treasury of the inner self, while an evil person produces evil from the evil treasury of the inner self. The inner self overflows with words that are spoken. – Luke 6:45

Looking at the Doctor, you wouldn't know that he is from another time and place. He looks human. He eats our food and breathes our air. He leaps for joy and weeps in lament. He gets angry and becomes fearful. He looks like you and me, except he isn't. Time Lords, such as the Doctor, have two hearts. Having two hearts is the physiological source of his incessant excitement and energy, but having two hearts means more than being able to outrun a bad guy or survive a grueling test. He's like us, but he's more. Dare I say that he is fully human and fully...Time Lord?

The Doctor certainly seems to be a Christ figure in the show, in much the same way that a superhero, such as Superman, always swoops in to save the day. Both are characters from somewhere far from the earth, who drop out of the sky with special powers only used for truth, justice, and all that is good. In some episodes, the Doctor's expression as a Christ figure is quite explicit. At the conclusion of "Last of the Time Lords,"[2] the Doctor's nemesis, the Master, seems to have delivered the Doctor a life-ending blow; but at the last moment, the Doctor is, in essence, resurrected. In the Doctor's final moment, through the help of his companion, Martha, all of humanity thinks of the Doctor at the same time, and their "belief" in him brings him back to life. Through this resurrection, he is able to save humanity from the Master's enslavement. The Doctor's faith in humanity is what, in turn, saves humanity itself, and the Doctor had to rely on humanity in order to save himself.

Salvation is not a one-way street. The gospel story shows us that salvation is rooted in relationship, especially when we think of Jesus' birth. It was quite an epiphany for me when I really considered the fact that Jesus had human parents. What was God thinking? Because being born into humanity certainly puts Jesus the baby in a vulnerable place. Professor and theologian Stanley Hauerwas writes:

To be human is to be vulnerable, but to be a baby is to be vulnerable in a manner we spend a lifetime denying. Indeed Jesus was a baby refusing to forego the vulnerability that would climax in his crucifixion. And as such, Jesus was entrusted to the care of Mary and Joseph. They could not save him from the crucifixion, but they were indispensable agents to making his life possible.[3]

God really surprises me sometimes. The Savior had parents. I've known this fact for quite awhile, but it took on new meaning when I became a parent myself. The Savior having parents sounds like a terrible plan. Parents don't always get it right. Parents don't always keep their composure. Parents forget things—um, when Jesus was twelve years old, Mary and Joseph left Jerusalem to head home, and it took them a full day to realize that Jesus wasn't with them! Some days I do all right, and other days I look up at the ceiling and say, "God, I wish I was better at this." What was God thinking when he decided to come to earth, and then rely on humanity in order to save humanity?

God, coming to earth "in-the-flesh," shows us that having faith actually makes us vulnerable. Faith is not a protective bubble against the dark places of the world. If it were, God would have never allowed himself to be raised by a pair of human, fallible, everyday parents. Jesus' birth and life reveal that God trusted humanity more than humanity has ever trusted itself: "God's righteousness is being revealed in the gospel, from faithfulness for faith, as it is written, *The righteous person will live by faith*" (Romans 1:17)—through faith for faith, Paul is saying. God had to trust in humanity in order to save humanity. What does it mean for God to trust in the broken, imperfect, screwed-up people of the world? To me it means that if God can trust in the midst of imperfection, I guess I can too.

In the two-part story, "Human Nature/Family of Blood,"[4] we learn about the time the Doctor actually loses one of his hearts. In these episodes, the Doctor uses a Chameleon Arch (which looks like a pretty fantastic pocket watch) to rewrite his own DNA from Time Lord to human in order to escape detection from "The Family," a telepathic entity seeking to feed off the Doctor's amazing ability to regenerate. The Doctor transforms his DNA and becomes a human hiding away as a schoolteacher, John Smith, at Farringham School for Boys in 1913 England.

Changing his DNA made it possible for the Doctor to hide, but becoming fully human has its shortcomings. First, the Doctor doesn't remember who he is. He has to rely on his season three companion, Martha Jones, to fill in the gaps. Martha, an actual doctor from twentieth-century London, first met the Doctor in the season opener, "Smith and Jones." Just before changing his DNA, the Doctor tells Martha that it is up to her to keep him out of sight, and that she must not reveal his true identity to anyone, even himself. Only when "The Family" has lost the trail is she to open the Chameleon Arch and transform him back. So, for most of the episode, the Doctor assumes that he is John Smith, an average schoolteacher living in 1913 England.

The second and more significant drawback to changing his DNA meant that it left the Doctor with only one heart. Having two hearts seems relatively unimportant to the Doctor's story, until the audience realizes what having an extra heart affords him—for one, the Doctor seems to be uninfluenced by any particular culture. For example, Martha Jones is a black woman. Her race is inconsequential to the Doctor, but through the early twentieth-century human eyes of John Smith, Martha is considered a lowly servant because of her race, only allowed to speak when spoken to. It seems that when the Doctor becomes fully human, he inherits our biases and missteps, losing his ability to rise above bigotry and fear. It appears that an abundance of hearts is what's needed to be critically empathetic and ethically good.

All in the Family

David Tennant, who played the Tenth Doctor, married Georgia Moffett, the daughter of the Fifth Doctor, Peter Davison, which surely made for some very confusing family reunions!

On the whole, the Doctor has two hearts. He looks like us, acts like us, and has spent so much time on the earth that he knows humanity better than it knows itself. Having two hearts means that the Doctor is a walking symbol of abundant grace. In a recent interview, head writer Steven Moffat said:

> When they made this particular superhero, they didn't give him a gun. They gave him a screwdriver to fix things. They didn't give him a tank or a warship or an X-Wing fighter, they gave him a call box from which you can call for help. And they didn't give him a superpower or pointy ears or a heat ray. They gave him an extra heart. They gave him two hearts. And that's an extraordinary thing; there will never come a time when we don't need a hero like the Doctor.[5]

His "cup runneth over" with compassion for the least and the lost. What would humanity be like if we had two hearts? The good news is that we don't have to guess. Being in Christ means that our heart works together with Christ's and with each other. When we come together as the body of Christ, we don't just have two hearts, but all of our hearts are united together in a beautiful vulnerability.

God had to rely on humanity in order to save humanity; therefore, we are called to trust in God and each other so that the world might be transformed for the good.

Is there someone in your life who is so kind that they seem to have "two hearts"? What makes them so kind?

What do you suppose Jesus' childhood was like? What do you think it means that our Savior had a childhood?

What breaks your heart? How might God be using that to call you into deeper relationship with him?

I NEVER FORGET A FACE

So if anyone is in Christ, there is a new creation: every-thing old has passed away; see, everything has become new!
— 2 Corinthians 5:17 NRSV

No doubt we've all gone through old photo albums and found pictures of ourselves and said, "I can't believe that was me!" If we sorted through your old boxes, maybe we'd find an unflattering middle school class picture or a Glamour Shots photo shoot you wish had never happened. Maybe you'd look back at the "old," who is young and fit and seems to be having fun, and think, *I really can't believe that was me.* While you can look at that ten-year-old picture and certainly claim you are the same person, the fascinating fact is that, biologically speaking, you actually aren't the same person you are today. A large percentage of the cells in the human body are replaced every seven to ten years, so your body has actually been regenerating and changing throughout those years, while weirdly keeping "you" intact.

One of the most interesting things about the Doctor is that he can regenerate. If the Doctor is mortally wounded, the cells in his body begin to rewrite themselves, and his body repairs itself by making a new one—at least, mostly. After the Doctor regenerates, he has a different appearance, a different personality, and different likes and dislikes (not to mention a different wardrobe). So, is he the same person? Most, including the Doctor, would say yes, but how can this be? (It should be said that regeneration is certainly a helpful trait for a television character to have. Contract dispute? New Doctor. The show needs to go in another direction? Change him out. The audience is trending this way or that? No worries! Mortally wound him and get a new one. The show must go on!)

Taking a look at each incarnation of the Doctor offers a window into the different personalities inside each and every one of us. The First Doctor, played by William Hartnell, was elderly and gruff, with little joy or patience for nonsense or frivolity. Taking the reins as the Second Doctor, Patrick Troughton assumed the role as a tragic clown of sorts, using a veiled incompetence to distract evildoers. The Third Doctor, Jon Pertwee, was a James Bond type of character—dashing and daring and always ready for hand-to-hand combat. The Doctor's fourth incarnation is one of the most endearing—for many, Tom Baker is the definitive Doctor (much like Sean Connery will always be the James Bond). He was quirky and quite alien, turning from joy to deep concern on a dime. (And who doesn't like Jellybabies, his favorite snack?) And the Fifth Doctor, Peter Davison, was handsome and compassionate and very human.[6]

31

The mold began to break with the sixth incarnation—Colin Baker's Doctor had a sharp wit and a sharper temper. Sylvester McCoy, the Seventh Doctor, began as a comical clown-like Doctor, but quickly became dark and somewhat manipulative. The eighth, Paul McGann, who has the shortest on-screen tenure to date, was arguably the most human Doctor—vulnerable and swayed by romantic love.[7] Christopher Eccleston's Doctor, the ninth, was reeling from the mass genocide of the Time War. Deeply depressed and perpetually hiding behind a false frivolity, he wore a leather jacket and played by his own rules. The Tenth Doctor, played by David Tennant, was apologetic and sincere, showing great power through humility and empathy. Matt Smith, the Eleventh Doctor, was whimsical and child-like, almost like a nutty Victorian professor. Finally, at least in this moment, the Twelfth Doctor, played by Peter Capaldi, is rather cold and calculating, with a dry humor and impatience with ignorance.

It is a bit unclear whether each Doctor expresses different personality traits that have always been with him, or whether with each regeneration the Doctor becomes, in essence, a new person. Becoming a new person, or being made new, is a concept familiar to those of us in the Christian faith. The apostle Paul writes:

> So then, from this point on we won't recognize people by human standards. Even though we used to know Christ by human standards, that isn't how we know him now. So then, if anyone is in Christ, that person is part of the new creation. The old things have gone away, and look, new things have arrived! (2 Corinthians 5:16–17)[8]

Jesus talks about being born again or being born from above (John 3:3) and putting new wine into new wineskins (Luke 5:38).

The Christian faith teaches that in Christ we are a new person, but nowhere does it say that becoming a new person only happens once! Praying Psalm 51:10, "Create a clean heart for me, God; / put a new, faithful spirit deep inside me!" is a prayer we should offer every day. Lamentations 3:22–23 says, "The faithful love of the LORD hasn't ended; / certainly God's compassion isn't through! / They are renewed every morning. / Great is your faithfulness." If God is meeting us each and every day with abundant mercy in Christ, perpetually offering us a new and right spirit, we are continually being made new.

Do you have a favorite Doctor? Why?

What does it mean to be made "new"?

Are you, in fact, the same person you were yesterday? What about ten years ago? How about thirty? Where do you draw the line?

RUN, YOU CLEVER BOY, AND REMEMBER

Remember me when you come into your kingdom.
— Luke 23:42

So when we say, "I," what are we really talking about? Why does the audience buy that the Twelfth Doctor is the same person as the others, even though he looks and thinks and acts different from all the others? Because the Doctor is able to remember all that he and his previous incarnations (or personas) have done in the past.

33

He remembers the story—the whole story—and so do we. His identity is rooted in our memories.

There is an intimate connection between memory and identity. This is why Jesus, on his last night with the disciples, said, "When you eat or drink, do this in remembrance of me." This is why after forty days and forty nights, God looked upon the ark, and the story says, "God remembered Noah," and the rains stopped. In Mark 8 Jesus is with the disciples and feeds four thousand people (vv. 1–10). Later in the chapter Jesus and the disciples get into a boat to go to the other side of the Sea of Galilee:

> Now the disciples had forgotten to bring any bread; and they had only one loaf with them....And [Jesus] cautioned them, saying, "Watch out—beware of the yeast of the Pharisees and the yeast of Herod." The disciples said to one another, "It is because we have no bread." And becoming aware of it, Jesus said to them, "Why are you talking about having no bread? Do you still not perceive or understand? Are your hearts hardened? Do you have eyes, and fail to see?...And do you not remember?" (vv. 14–17 NRSV)

In other words, Jesus is asking, "Have you so quickly forgotten what I can do?"

We are a narrative. We are a story. We are more than what we think, say, or do. We *are* what we think, say, *and* do...*over time.* That is why it is essential for our stories to be surrounded by God's story. We are close to the heart of God when we remember that our story is no longer about us, but is a part of Christ's story. This is why what Paul says in Galatians 2 is so profound—"I have been crucified with Christ. It is no longer I who live, but Christ who lives in me" (v. 20 ESV).

Now we may disagree our identity is our memories, but my point is that whatever it is you consider "I" to be, whatever you see in your mind's eye when you say your name, whatever that image is, the point is for "I" to be crucified so that Christ may live within us. In other words, my prayer is that "I" reflects Jesus Christ. The "I" has been redeemed. Our thoughts, our words, our deeds, our time... all of it has been reconciled to God through Jesus Christ because by the power of the Holy Spirit, Christ is living within us. What will be eternal is the part of who I am that is joined with Christ—the part of me that has compassion for the poor, that feeds the hungry, that blesses children, that spends time apart with God, that restores sight to those who are blind, that seeks justice, that walks on the "other side" of the lake and so forth. All that which is not connected with the Spirit of Christ will be burned away and forgotten (see Malachi 3:1–4).

Christ has been resurrected. Christ ascended into heaven. By the power of the Holy Spirit, all that is within me that is connected with Christ also is resurrected and ascends into heaven. This is what Paul means when he says in Romans 6:

> Therefore, we were buried together with him through baptism into his death, so that just as Christ was raised from the dead through the glory of the Father, we too can walk in newness of life. If we were united together in a death like his, we will also be united together in a resurrection like his. This is what we know: the person that we used to be was crucified with him in order to get rid of the corpse that had been controlled by sin. That way we wouldn't be slaves to sin anymore, because a person who has died has been freed from sin's power. But if we died with Christ, we have faith that we will also live with him. We know that Christ has

been raised from the dead and he will never die again. Death no longer has power over him. He died to sin once and for all with his death, but he lives for God with his life. In the same way, you also should consider yourselves dead to sin but alive for God in Christ Jesus. (vv. 4–11)

There is an intimate connection between our memory and what we consider to be real. Consider a distant memory from your childhood that fades over time. Let's say when you were in the third grade you remember accidentally pulling the fire alarm outside of your classroom. It was the single most exciting event of the entire year for you and your friends. Years later you retell the story and find that not everyone remembers what happened, or at least the story is told differently. Again years pass, fewer remember what happened, and then there comes a day when neither you nor anyone else remembers the story. If no one remembers an event, can we say with certainty that it happened?

Throughout season five, the Doctor notices that there are "cracks" in the universe—something dramatic is ripping apart the fabric of space and time, and it all seems to be centered around his new companion, Amy Pond. At the end of the season, the Doctor discovers that someone has blown up the TARDIS, causing the universe to splinter. All of time is collapsing in on itself, erasing everything that has ever happened. In order to stop the process, the Doctor decides to reboot the entire universe using the light from a device called the Pandorica. It is to be the "big bang part two." The catch is that, in order for anything to pop back into existence, Amy must remember it because the tear in the universe was focused around her.

The Doctor flies the Pandorica into the heart of the exploding TARDIS, and the universe reboots in a fantastic explosion. However, during the reboot, the Doctor's life is moving in reverse, and he will soon be trapped outside of this universe of Amy's memory. Before he goes, he sees her as a child and whispers a story to her saying, "When you wake up…you won't remember me. I'll just be a story in your head, but that's ok. We're all stories in the end. Just make it a good one."[9] He then tells her about his time machine, the TARDIS. He said that he had borrowed it. It was big and little at the same time, both ancient and new in the same moment, and it was the bluest of blues. Of course, in great *Doctor Who* fashion, the Doctor pops back into existence on Amy's wedding day, when she is reminded of the old wedding tradition of "Something old, something new, something borrowed, something blue."

Here's the good news: we have been given the opportunity to live our lives with Christ, and walking with Christ throughout our lives is a means of remembering salvation, literally to re-member or to bring back God's life-giving spirit into our lives. But salvation is not all about us being able to remember—it's about us being *remembered by* God through Christ in the power of the Spirit. I think the thief on the cross in the Gospel of Luke got it right! He looked at Jesus and simply said, "Remember me when you come into your kingdom," to which Christ says, "I assure you that today you will be with me in paradise" (Luke 23:42, 43).

Our memories fail. We try to walk with Christ, but we make countless mistakes and missteps along the way. How wonderful to know that my salvation doesn't lie in my ability to remember Christ but rests in the grace of Christ to remember me.

What is your earliest memory, and what does that memory have to do with who you are now?

What would you hope Jesus "remembers" about your story? What do you hope Jesus might forget?

THE OLDEST QUESTION

But Moses said to God, "If I now come to the Israelites and say to them, 'The God of your ancestors has sent me to you,' they are going to ask me, 'What's this God's name?' What am I supposed to say to them?" – Exodus 3:13

What's in a name? The greatest mystery in *Doctor Who* is the Doctor's actual name. Except for the Doctor and his wife, River Song, no one knows his real name.[10] Throughout most of season six, the Doctor is fighting a religious order called "The Silence," who wants him dead. He receives word that there is a prophecy about a mysterious question that should never be answered. At the end of the season, the Doctor has figured out what the question is, though the audience is not made aware of it until a galactic businessman, Dorium, calls out to the Doctor as he's walking off screen: "The first question—the question that must never be answered, hidden in plain sight. The question you've been running from all your life. Doctor who?"[11]

"The Doctor" is a title that he has chosen for himself. He sees himself as a healer, and one that fights for goodness throughout the universe. His chosen name is a pledge, of sorts—"Never cruel, nor cowardly. Never give up. Never give in."[12] The Doctor wrestles with keeping this promise, especially when he is forced to make difficult choices for the greater good. After fully committing to the pledge, he tucked away his name, only to offer it once to his wife on his wedding day (at least we think). So, "the Doctor" might as well be his name.

Names are important to our identities. I remember how my wife and I got stuck when we were thinking about baby names for our second daughter. We just could not agree on a name. My wife really liked the name "Greenleigh," after Joni Mitchell's song "Little Green," but for me, naming my daughter a colorful adverb was just out of the question. (Of course, all of the names I wanted were perfect—so perfect, in fact, that I won't mention them here.) Finally we decided to take my wife's middle name, my oldest daughter's middle name, and my middle name, and put them all together. Soon Annaleigh Berke was welcomed into the world.

Throughout Scripture, names are layered with meaning. *Jesus* in Hebrew means "God saves," which pretty much sums it up, right? Jesus was born in Bethlehem, which means "House of Bread," reminding us that Christ is the bread of life that feeds us at the Communion table. Jesus lived in Nazareth, which means "new shoot," pointing us to the new covenant that will spring up from Jesus' life, death, and resurrection. God put on flesh in the person of Jesus in order to save God's people—called *Israel* throughout Scripture. The name *Israel* was introduced when Jacob met the Lord (in the form of an angel) and wrestled with him all night: "He said to Jacob, 'What's your name?' and he said, 'Jacob.' Then he said, 'Your name won't be Jacob any longer, but Israel, because you struggled with God and with men and won.'" (Genesis 32:27–28).

Israel in Hebrew means, "One who wrestles with God and humanity and prevails." It was a fitting name, given that Jacob had wrestled with his past. After Jacob deceived their father and stole his brother's birthright and blessing, Esau vowed revenge. So Jacob ran away, hoping his brother would calm down and it would all blow over. Have you ever run from a problem, thinking that maybe time would bring healing? Have you ever avoided difficult, but needed, conversations?

Jacob fled, but time and distance didn't erase the past. Years later, Jacob finally decided to meet his brother. He sent his family across the Jordan River ahead of him (was this a cowardly move?) and lingered alone with his thoughts. An angel appeared to him and wrestled with him all night, the two locked in what must have felt like an epic battle. I imagine that with each passing moment, with each twist and grip, with teeth gnashing and tension building, the Lord was offering Jacob forgiveness. In the end, the angel blessed Jacob, but he wasleft with a permanent limp. He was forgiven, but never the same. Afterward, he crossed the river to meet his brother. When Esau saw Jacob, "Esau ran to meet him, threw his arms around his neck, kissed him, and they wept" (Genesis 33:4).

What a beautifully authentic image of our relationship with the Divine and with each other. God's people are not those who simply live in blind faith, shiny happy people who do no wrong. Like Jacob, God's people are those who choose to wrestle with faith, those who fight the good fight of justice with mercy. God's people are those who struggle against the narrative that says having more stuff will make us happy. God's people are those who wrestle with who God is and what God is calling us to become. Jesus came to save Israel—God's people, who wrestle with loving God and loving each other.

The most important name in Scripture is God's name. When Moses stands before the burning bush and, like Jacob, asks God, "What is your name?" the Lord replies, "I Am Who I Am" (Exodus 3:14). In other words, God's name means, "to be." God is what it means to be alive. As a child of God, what does your name mean? Do you even know? Does your name fit who you consider yourself to be? If you were able to choose a title describing who you are, what would your title be? Maybe a better question is, "What title do you aspire to?" Can you pledge, "Never cruel or cowardly. Never give in. Never give up"? Maybe being Israel—God's chosen—is enough.

Maybe wrestling with God and each other is enough. The good news is that God has already given you a title—"wonderfully made" (Psalm 139:14 NRSV). Rest in the hope and the peace that whether you wrestle with God or turn away from grace, God is the author of us all.

How can you live up to God's calling of being "wonderfully made"?

What titles do you use to describe those around you? Do you see others as being wonderfully made?

If you could write yourself a pledge to live by, what would it be?

Chapter Two

GOD AND TIME AND GOD'S TIME

God said, "Let there be lights in the dome of the sky to separate the day from the night. They will mark events, sacred seasons, days and years." – Genesis 1:14

Time is a strange thing. Have you ever felt that time seems to stop on a Friday afternoon, but the weekend never seems long enough? Maybe you can't quite remember what life was like before you met your significant other, though you only met a few years ago. Or have you ever had a dream that felt as though it lasted for hours, but you were actually only sleeping for twenty minutes?

Out of all of God's creations, time seems to be one of the most powerful and one of the most curious. We can defy gravity, cure diseases, harness solar energy, desalinate water, but we are all bound by the same twenty-four hours of each day. Time is so powerful, and so outside of our grasp, that we have yet to discover a way to defy it or turn it around or speed it up.

How I wish I had a time machine. It would be awesome to have the ability to go back in time and fix some of my mistakes; but when you stop to think about it, isn't this what God does when we ask for forgiveness? Have you ever thought about the relationship between salvation and time? And how is it that God can forgive my past anyway? If God can see all of time, when I get to heaven, will I be able to do the same? Will I be able to look down on myself as a young man and watch myself make mistakes?

When Christians talk about salvation, words like *eternal* and *everlasting* and *forever* come up. But just how long is eternal life? I mean, I love eating buffalo wings, but I'm not sure I want to eat them for all eternity. I'm not sure even what I would love to do for all time, outside of being in the presence of God. Maybe that's the point.

Jesus doesn't seem to worry a whole lot about time. He said things like, "Stop worrying about tomorrow, because tomorrow will worry about itself. Each day has enough trouble of its own" (Matthew 6:34). When Jesus hears about Lazarus being ill, Jesus lingers for two days before finally heading down to Bethany saying, "This illness isn't fatal. It's for the glory of God so that God's Son can be glorified through it" (John 11:4). Jesus heals on the sabbath day, a day set apart for no work; but on other days he goes off by himself and just lets the world seemingly spin without him. He just doesn't seem bound by time like the rest of us. Maybe we should take a cue from him and learn how to step away from everything from time to time to recharge. In fact, maybe you'd even be willing to turn off your iPhone for a few minutes and do just that … at least long enough to read this chapter.

WHEN TIME BEGAN

I've always been curious as to why there seems to be a divide between science and faith. The creation accounts in Scripture (Genesis 1–2) are sometimes used to by two separate camps to explain exactly how the universe began. In general, Creationists claim that God created everything seen and unseen, as detailed in Scripture. Evolutionists suggest that life came about through happenstance and evolved to match a constantly changing environment. Even though hard-liners on either side seem immovable, they actually both agree on at least one thing— in order for life to be, water must be present. The first few verses of Scripture reveal, "When God began to create the heavens and the earth—the earth was without shape or form, it was dark over the deep sea, and God's wind swept over the waters" (Genesis 1:1–2). The story suggests that water is already present when God begins to create.

Carefully reading the rest of the creation account reveals even more common ground between the two immutable camps. First, consider the order in which God creates. There is first light, then sea and land, then vegetation, fish, animals, and then people. This order roughly resembles how biologists and geologists suggest things came to be. Second, and more important, God creates through permission. God allows the earth to bring forth life. For example, "God said, 'Let the waters swarm with living things, and let birds fly above the earth up in the dome of the sky'" (Genesis 1:20) and "God said, 'Let the earth produce every kind of living thing: livestock, crawling things, and wildlife.' And that's what happened" (v. 24).

Yes, God is the Creator, and Scripture reveals that God created through permission. In these few paragraphs I don't mean to end the debate, but maybe both sides of the story do have more in common with each other when we shift our focus away from the self and look to God and the world God created.

THE BIG BANG

God said, "Let there be light." And so light appeared.
— Genesis 1:3

Have you ever considered just exactly what time is, or how long a moment might be? Why does a tragedy seem to move in slow motion, but a good time just flies by?

Time is a measurement, much like length or width or height. Time is simply an expression of duration, or in my case, it is the duration between when one cup of coffee ends and the next begins. You see, time doesn't make sense unless you can observe something in constant repetition. The sun comes up; the sun goes down. Winter brings snow; summer brings sunshine.

But what would it be like to live outside of time? In "The Wedding of River Song," at the end of *Doctor Who's* sixth season, time becomes "stuck," and as a result, the universe begins to disintegrate. All of history—both past and future—collides, and all kinds of crazy events start happening at once. Roman chariots stop at streetlights, and flying cars buzz by the Great Pyramid of Giza. Time begins to fold in on itself, and the universe is on the edge of collapsing altogether. (Until the Doctor figures out a way to save the day, of course.)

Though our lives are very much dictated by time, it's amazing to think about how God is not. In Revelation 22:13 he says, "I am the alpha and the omega, the first and the last, the beginning and the end." God is *omnipresent*, meaning he is present at all times, in all places, all at once, which is pretty mind-boggling when you stop to think about it. In the beginning, when God created the heavens and the earth (see Genesis 1), there was no such thing as time, as we know it. Some read Genesis 1 literally, and say that Creation happened in seven, twenty-four hour days. Fair enough. Even though Scripture doesn't specifically offer a daily time frame of these events, it does say there was an evening and a morning, marking a relative beginning and ending of God's creative action each "day."

It is not until "day four" of Creation that God creates time as we know it. On that day God said, "Let there be lights in the dome of the sky to separate the day from the night. They will mark events, sacred seasons, days, and years. They will be lights in the dome of the sky to shine on the earth" (Genesis 1:14–15). So time was a part of Creation—just like fish or ferns or physics. Time is God's gift to us so that we might know when to plant and when to harvest, when to wake and when to rest.

RESOLUTE RIVALS

There are more than forty ways to defeat a Dalek, yet these creatures remain one of the Doctor's most insistent foes.

Time is a great example of God's grace. Each and every one of us—whether saint or sinner, prince or pauper—have all been given twenty-four hours a day. How do you accept this gift of time? Does it feel like a grace or a burden to you? If I asked you, what one hour of your time is worth, how would you answer? Would you think about how many tasks you could get done in that time or how much money you could earn? Chances are, you could easily come up with a dollar amount to that question. It's the way our world operates, right? But when God placed the sun in the sky, I'm not sure that he intended humanity to be so quick to assign each hour a monetary value. Nowhere during the six days of Creation did it say, "And God said, 'Let there be money so that humanity knows what its time is worth.' "

We seem to be "stuck" in time, so to speak. For us, time only moves in one direction—toward the future. There is no going back, so moving forward is the only option. Because this is such a part of who we are, it's hard to think of time any different. This is one of the reasons why I think *Doctor Who* is so much fun to watch—the audience is never stuck in time. During the Matt Smith seasons (and one of David Tennant's tenure), the Doctor and River Song's time lines are happening in reverse (both are time travelers and apparently married). In the two-part episode "Silence in the Library/Forest of the Dead,"[1] the Doctor sees River for the first time, but you come to find out that it's the last time that River sees the Doctor...well, sort of. Each time we see them onscreen, the audience has no idea where each is in each other's time line. In another episode, "Day of the Moon,"[2] River and the Doctor are saying goodbye to each other. She grabs his tweed jacket and kisses him passionately as he awkwardly reacts. After their embrace River notices that the Doctor seems curiously shocked. The Doctor replies that there is a first time for everything, and River is saddened, realizing that his first kiss with her is her last kiss with him.

The future is unknown to all of us, but is it unknown to God? Does God know the future? In a word, yes, but maybe not in the way we might expect. For example, if I put an open cookie jar in front of my young daughter, I know what she's going to do. I know she's going to reach her hand into the jar to get a cookie. Does that mean I can tell the future? Hardly. But it does mean that I know my daughter better than she knows herself. So, does God know the future? I'm not sure, but I do know that God knows us better than we know ourselves. As Psalm 139:1–6 reads:

> Lord, you have examined me.
> You know me.

You know when I sit down.
   And when I stand up.
   Even from far away,
     You comprehend my plans.
You study my traveling and resting.
     You are thoroughly familiar with all my ways.
There isn't a word on my tongue, Lord,
     That you don't already know completely.
You surround me—front and back.
     You put your hand on me.
That kind of knowledge
   Is too much for me.
     It's so high above me that I can't fathom it.

So, if God knows us better than we know ourselves, can we ever surprise God? I think so. God knows the future in the sense that God knows all that is possible, but there is room for surprise. Think of it this way. God knows every possible way to get from Los Angeles to New York, but whether I take a right or a left out of my driveway at the beginning of my road trip is undetermined. Have you ever tried to surprise God for the good? Maybe you always worry about money. Try surprising God by putting your worry away (see Matthew 6:25). Maybe you never begin your mornings with prayer. What a pleasant surprise to talk to God first thing before the sun rises! God knows us better than we know ourselves. God knows where the story is headed, and yet God graciously invites us into the story as active participants.

If you could go back in time and change one thing, what would it be?

*And because you can't go back in time and change the past,
what is the best way you can use your time today? How can you
surprise God for the good today?*

AN UNCAUSED EFFECT

*"People assume that time is a strict progression of cause to
effect, but actually from a non-linear, non-subjective
viewpoint—it's more like a big ball of wibbly-wobbly…
time-y wimey…stuff."[3] – The Doctor to Sally Sparrow*

It's not just the Doctor and River Song who play with time's
proverbial flow. Scripture breaks down our assumptions about what
we think we know of the world. Most people assume that time moves
in one direction—from cause to effect, but in actuality this is not the
case. The story of Jesus' transfiguration[4] offers us a possible glimpse
into the wibbly-wobbliness of time. Scripture says that Jesus climbed
the mountain with Peter, James, and John, and he was transfigured
before them, meaning that his clothes became a dazzling white and his
appearance changed. It's something you just don't see everyday.

Jesus, transfigured, is seen standing with Moses and Elijah (both
deceased), surrounded by a bright cloud. From where are Moses and
Elijah speaking with Jesus? Are they in heaven? Is Jesus speaking
with them from Sheol, the Hebrew land of the dead? Did Moses
and Elijah become one with The Force, making them able to appear
as phantoms? Scripture doesn't say, though becoming one with The
Force is really unlikely. Maybe there's something even deeper going
on here.

Both Moses and Elijah also had mountaintop experiences with God. In 1 Kings 19, Elijah is out in the wilderness running from King Ahab, who wants to kill him. The Lord cries out to Elijah asking him, "Why are you here, Elijah?" "Go out and stand at the mountain before the Lord. The Lord is passing by" (1 Kings 19:9, 11). Elijah climbs a mountain and finds a small cave where he can hide. There is a great wind, but God is not in the wind. There is a great earthquake, but God is not in the earthquake. There is a great fire, but God is not in the fire. Then there is the "sound of sheer silence" (19:12 NRSV).

Many years before Elijah, Moses also climbed a mountain. (See Exodus 19.) Like Elijah, Moses experienced an earthquake and fire on his trek, and the glory of the Lord was so great that Moses' face radiated with a holy glow. Elijah went up with a question—"Why are you here?" Moses came down with answers—ten of them, in fact. I'm curious, though. Moses went up the mountain, and there was an earthquake and fire and smoke. Elijah went up the mountain, and there was an earthquake and fire and a great wind. Jesus climbed the mountain and was transfigured, speaking to both Moses and Elijah. It makes me wonder if our biblical authors are recording the same event. Maybe the glory that Moses saw was the transfigured Christ? Maybe the conversation Elijah was having with the Lord was Jesus asking him, "Why are you here?"

Time doesn't move in the same way with God as it does with us. Maybe the point of these three stories (and with the Transfiguration, your guess is as good as mine) is to know that God in Christ is always with us. Whether we go up the mountain for the answers, or we go up the mountain with a good question, or we go up the mountain simply because Jesus asked us to go, maybe the point of it all is that God is always with us.

In the episode "Blink,"[5] the Doctor finds himself stuck in 1969 without his time machine (the TARDIS). He and his companion,

Martha, had been sent back into the past by alien beings known as Weeping Angels, and are forced to find a way to communicate with someone in the future so they can get the TARDIS back and return. In the episode's opening scene, the character Sally Sparrow is exploring an old, abandoned house when she discovers some curious scribbling behind a wallpaper corner. As she tears the paper away, she finds a series of warnings written directly to her from "the Doctor"—a person she has never met. Throughout the episode, Sally finds more clues that the Doctor has left for her, almost as if he knew where she would be and when.

Soon Sally meets Larry Nightingale, a local DVD rental shop worker, who has been uncovering "Easter eggs" in a random selection of movies. ("Easter eggs" are messages or extras that are hidden in movies or films, like the Pizza Planet truck that always appears somewhere in Pixar movies.) In these movies, Larry has discovered Easter eggs of a strange man talking to the camera, and has put the messages together in what he assumes to be the correct order. When he shows Sally the list of movies containing the messages, she realizes that the list precisely matches her home DVD collection.

Sally and Larry go back to the abandoned house to watch the full message put together; and to her astonishment, Sally realizes that the man in the video—the Doctor—seems to be having a real-time conversation with her, which appears to be impossible. The Doctor tells her that it seems that they are interacting because he knows everything that she is going to say. Almost ominously, the Doctor tells her to look to her left, where Sally sees that Larry is writing a transcript of their conversation. The same transcript was given to the Doctor at some point in the future, and he brought it back to the past so that their present "conversation" could happen.

Still with me? I don't blame you if you're lost and confused at this point. Sally certainly was, which is why the Doctor offered his best explanation of the nature of time—"People assume that time is a strict progression of cause to effect, but actually from a non-linear, non-subjective viewpoint—it's more like a big ball of wibbly-wobbly...time-y wimey...stuff."[6]

We often assume that time flows in one direction from cause to effect, but this cannot be the case. Let's assume that every effect has a cause, or "A" causes "B," which causes "C," and so on. For example, imagine you are at a dinner party. Someone tells a really great joke about a pickle, a Dalmatian, and a funny-smelling shoe. You laugh so hard you knock your water glass off the table with your elbow, and it shatters into pieces. Cause and effect would look like this: You laugh at the joke (A), you knock the glass with your elbow (B), and then the glass shatters when it hits the floor (C). The problem is, if you rewind the clock you discover that, at some point, you run across an uncaused effect. The joke made you laugh, but who told the joke? Who told the joke to them? So on and so forth. If you look closely, you'll eventually discover the moment in which something happened from nothing. It is specifically *not* the case that our world moves *only* from cause to effect.

So, what does an uncaused effect look like? The church some-times calls them miracles. It looks like water being turned into wine. It looks like feeding five thousand people from a young boy's lunch of fish and loaves. It looks like Jesus being transfigured on the mountain talking with Moses and Elijah in defiance of our simple cause-to-effect world. God is the uncaused effect—action with no beginning and no end; and when God enters into our world, we are reminded of how marvelously and strangely beautiful God's world is. When we worship a risen Lord, when we live as if our story ends with everlasting life, the rules of the world do not apply.

The Weeping Angels feed off of lost potential. Have you ever experienced a missed opportunity? How did you move forward?

Does understanding miracles as "uncaused effects" make it easier or more difficult to believe in them?

If you were to make a time capsule detailing your life over the last year, what would you be sure to include?

MOVING AT THE SPEED OF SALVATION

I am the light of the world. Whoever follows me won't walk in darkness but will have the light of life. – John 8:12

Several years ago, when I was praying about whether God was calling me to be a pastor, I had a vivid dream. I dreamed I was standing outside of the eastern wall in Jerusalem, surrounded by shadowy figures. I saw a light in the distance calling out to me; and as I came closer to the light, I realized that the light was Jesus himself. I saw Jesus standing among the shadows. Interestingly, the closer I came to the light, the less I could see. The light was blinding to me until Jesus asked me to turn around. Immediately my vision improved, and I could see that the shadows were other people who were standing in awe of Christ. Instead of staring at the light, I allowed the light to illuminate what was around me. In other words, Jesus wasn't calling me to stare at him—he was calling me to see my neighbor. Ever since that vision, I have been fascinated with Christ's connection with light.

The more I think about light, the more I appreciate how perfect a metaphor it is for Christ. The Gospel of John begins,

> In the beginning was the Word,
>> and the Word was with God
>> and the Word was God....
> What came into being
>> through the Word was life,
>> and the life was the light for all people.
> The light shines in the darkness,
>> and the darkness doesn't extinguish the light."
>>> (John 1:1, 3–5)

Christ was in the beginning with God. When God looked upon a dark and formless world, God created light to shine in the darkness, and that light was Christ.

If that's not cool enough, much of the Apostle John's account of Jesus' resurrection happens in the midst of darkness. John records, "Early in the morning of the first day of the week, while it was still dark, Mary Magdalene came to the tomb" (John 20:1). Later that evening Jesus appeared again, this time to the disciples who were hiding behind locked doors. In both cases, Jesus appeared in the midst of darkness, once again proving John's words—"The light shines in the darkness, / and the darkness doesn't extinguish the light" (John 1:5).

ANCIENT MYSTERY SOLVED

According to *Doctor Who*, the Loch Ness monster is a Skarasen, a creature left here in the twelfth century by the alien race of Zygons, who were pursuing world domination.

Now, I am certainly no physicist, but what I know about darkness is that it can't overcome light because light is the constant and timeless boundary of the universe, which is why it is such a perfect metaphor for Christ. Nothing travels faster than light; and if it did, it would be flung out of the universe like an unlucky child who didn't hold on to the merry-go-round when her mischievous big brother had the chance to spin it. The speed of light is the great constant of the universe. No matter how fast or slow you are traveling, light travels at the constant speed of 299,792,458 meters per second. If you were able to approach this fantastic speed, a few strange things would happen to you. You would notice that all of the weight you lost just in time for swimsuit season has come back with a vengeance, because the closer you come to the speed of light, the greater your mass becomes.

Not only would you gain mass, but you would also notice that the second hand on your watch hadn't moved in a while because as you approach the speed of light, time slows down. Think of it as Einstein did. One day he was simply looking at a clock. He started to think that if he traveled away from the clock at the speed of light, he would never see the second hand move. Because in order to see the clock, light must bounce off the clock and into our eyes. And if we move away from the clock at the speed of light, light doesn't have the chance to enter our eyes; therefore, time itself would seem to stop. You would also become effectively invisible, which is pretty cool too.

Light is timeless. The entire universe is bound by its consistency. Scripture tells us that everything was made through Christ, and without Christ nothing would be (see John 1:3). Christ was in the beginning with God, and will be with God in the end. Christ is the light of the world, not only because through Christ we find the way, the truth, and the life, but because he is the timeless boundary of all that it is; and much like there is more "you" as you approach the speed of light, the closer we come to Christ, the more we discover who God is calling us to be. With eyes of physics and faith, these are the rules.

The Doctor has rules too. I wouldn't say the Doctor is a religious person, but he does have rules that define how he understands the universe. In the two-part series "The Impossible Planet/The Satan Pit," the Doctor's rules are challenged when he comes across a being that says it existed before the universe. This troubles the Doctor because this creature's existence doesn't fit his rules, not to mention that this creature threatens the life of every living thing (as per the typical episode). As the Doctor investigates, someone asks him if he is a man of faith. He thinks to himself out loud that this creature doesn't fit his rules for the universe, but that he keeps traveling in order to be proved wrong.

The Doctor travels through all of time and space just so that his rules might be proved wrong. What are your rules? Do you go through life hoping that you'll be proved right, or think that only your opinion is important? When Jesus is a part of our lives, it turns our assumptions upside down—the last shall be first, Samaritans are good, the prodigal is welcomed, and the poor are blessed. As a Christian, the only correct assumption is "Christ is Lord." If you believe that Christ is the timeless boundary of all that is, how does that affect the way you see the world or your neighbor or your checkbook or where you live or the importance of your favorite team winning the championship? Which of our assumptions need to change? Like the Doctor, are you willing to travel in order to be proved wrong? Are you willing to walk with Christ so that all you know of the world might be seen in a new light?

What are the "rules" you live by?

How has your understanding of God changed over the years?

*Light is one of the most powerful images representing Christ.
What other images for Christ resonate with you?*

THE CROSS AND RELATIVITY

*He reconciled all things to himself through him—
whether things on earth or in the heavens.
He brought peace through the blood of his cross.*
— Colossians 1:20

When I was young, my family would attend a camp meeting with my grandmother's church every October. We would gather with other churchgoers in a tin-roof, open-air sanctuary for an entire week of worship, fellowship, and the best soul food in the South. The Sunday afternoon service was the highlight of the week, though. The music was loud and the sermon was long, but the altar call surpassed them both in decibel and duration.

My Uncle Ronnie faithfully attended these meetings every year, and I often sat next to him. To say he was a saint is probably an exaggeration, but you could say I got saved because of him—if he felt the altar call was going on longer than it should, he would give me five dollars to go and get saved so the service would end already. Having attended years and years of camp meetings during my youth, I'd say I've probably been saved more than most. Jesus said, "What will people give in exchange for their lives?" (Mark 8:37). According to Uncle Ronnie, it's about five bucks.

A lot of people get very concerned about being able to pinpoint the exact moment that they were "saved." For some, this time and date stamp is very important, while others think of their salvation as more of a journey than an event. The Doctor describes time as a wibbly-wobbly ball of stuff. That's a pretty fair description, I think. You see, time only makes sense when there is a relationship between more than one object. Time is an expression of relationship. For example, let's imagine that you and I sync our iPhones so that they read the exact same time. If we remain moving at about the same speed, our phones will agree on what time it is. But if we begin to move at different speeds closer or farther apart, and one of us is moving much faster than the other, the clock app on our phones will no longer agree. Why is that? Because GPS satellites orbiting in space move at a different speed than we do on earth; they have their own unit of time measurement. If the GPS is to be able to tell you when you will arrive at a destination, it has to correct for our different rates of time. So, yeah, as the Doctor put it, time is wibbly-wobbly—or if you prefer Einstein's theory, it's relative.

So since salvation is rooted in a relationship with God through Christ in the power of the Holy Spirit, what is the relationship between salvation and time? Some have asked me, "If Jesus died in A.D. 33, what about the folks who died in A.D. 32? Did they miss the salvation boat? Are they just out of luck?" I say no! It's easy for our logical minds to go down this path, but Scripture tells us that the mystery of the cross is that it works both ways:

> He reconciled all things to himself through him—
> whether things on earth or in the heavens.
> > He brought peace through the blood of his cross.
> > > (Colossians 1:20)

God reconciled *all* things—including time—so that time itself is simply an agent of the gospel.

One of the most beautiful and amazing things about the Bible is that the entire Bible tells the story of Jesus and the gospel—from the very beginning to the very end. Throughout the Old Testament—written way before Jesus was born—there are countless stories that foretell Jesus' birth, his life, and his death on the cross. For example, we learn in the New Testament that Jesus was crucified and then, *on the third day*, defeated sin and death and was resurrected. In the Old Testament, we see many examples of "on the third day." On *the third day* Abraham saw the place where he was to sacrifice Isaac (Genesis 22:4). The ancient Israelites were at the foot of Mount Sinai and on *the third day*, there was thunder and lightning and the sound of trumpets (Exodus 19:16). The Philistines captured the ark of the covenant, but on *the third day* the ark began its journey back to God's chosen people (1 Samuel 5).

How can our concept of time moving steadily forward be so different from God's? It's like in the episode, "The Girl Who Waited,"[7] when the Doctor, Amy, and Rory travel to the planet Apalapucia, one of the greatest vacation destinations in the entire universe. When they arrive, the Doctor and Rory get separated from Amy. They are finally able to communicate with her through a looking-glass type of communicator, but when they lose connection with her momentarily, they discover that Amy's time stream is moving much faster than theirs. They lost connection for a few seconds, but for her it had been a week since she had last spoken with them. Rory and the Doctor immediately hop in the TARDIS to save Amy, and their journey back to her only takes a few seconds. But for Amy, she had been left alone for forty years.

It's not that our clock moves faster than God's or that God's moves faster than ours; it's that God is independent of time, which means that when we talk about God, using a time line doesn't make much sense. For instance, consider forgiveness. When you think of it, asking for forgiveness is an exercise in time travel—we *presently* confess our sins, in the *future* hope that God will forgive our *past*. The fact that God is independent of time is the very reason forgiveness is possible! That's why the folk who died in A.D. 32 are not necessarily out of luck. God reconciled all things, which includes time itself. Through Jesus, God redeems the past and offers a new future. Time is not a hurdle in receiving God's gift of salvation. God's mercy and love is even greater than time itself.

So was I "saved" every time Uncle Ronnie gave me five dollars to head up to the altar? I don't know. Maybe. Sometimes people ask me to name the day I was saved, and my answer has always been, "Roundabout A.D. 33." I think some are too quick in their tendency to plot out salvation on a time line, suggesting that we aren't truly in Christ unless we do A, B, then C. I just don't think that's how God works. I believe salvation is a process, the courage to live into the "ball of stuff" of God's grace. Paul said, "But when the fullness of time had come, God sent his Son" (Galatians 4:4 NRSV). That means that *whenever* we seek God, we experience his fullness and timelessness.

I often preach about God's grace as being "prevenient," meaning that God loves us even before we are aware of who God is, much in the same way that a parent cares for a child long before the child is even aware that he is in need. It means that God moves toward us before we move toward God, but in actuality, that "before" or "after" only makes sense from our limited perspective. If we are children of God, he is present and working in us throughout our entire lives, regardless if we can circle the date we first realized it. Scripture says that in Christ all things are made new (2 Corinthians 5:17 NRSV), but "new" is a word that only makes sense when you're stuck in time.

Maybe when Jesus talks about being made new, his "new" is really an eternal "now."

What is your salvation story? Can you pinpoint an exact moment you felt close to Christ? Is your story a journey rather than a specific moment?

In your own words, how can you best describe what Paul means when he says that God has "reconciled all things" through Christ?

What do you think it means to be made new in Christ?

THE ETERNAL NOW

Dear friends, now we are God's children, and it hasn't yet appeared what we will be. We know that when he appears we will be like him because we'll see him as he is.
                                               – 1 John 3:2

I was once visiting with a fellow pastor when I noticed something curious in his sanctuary. The sanctuary walls were lined with beautiful stained glass windows depicting Jesus' life, but I immediately noticed something was missing—there was no Resurrection window. When I asked the pastor about it, he said, "Well, there is a Resurrection window," pointing out a window detailing Jesus feeding Peter around a charcoal fire. This picture certainly told part of the Resurrection story (found in John 21), but based on the way the windows were arranged around the sanctuary—telling Jesus' life from birth to death—the window was out of place. It appeared before the Crucifixion window that depicted Jesus' death. *How embarrassing is that?* I thought to myself. But what the pastor said next stopped me in my tracks: "We were too busy with building the sanctuary, too busy with the unnecessary things of the world, that we failed to recognize the Resurrection. We thought about fixing the window, but we decided to leave it so that it's a constant reminder to never again miss the Resurrection."

NEW BEGINNINGS

When the Doctor regenerates, it's not only his appearance that changes—often the TARDIS and Sonic Screwdriver get makeovers too. There have been six different TARDIS designs, nine different Sonic Screwdrivers, and eleven different TARDIS control rooms.

Jesus feeding Peter around a charcoal fire is the Gospel of John's way of talking about the Resurrection. One of the really interesting things about John is that his Gospel is arranged in much the same way as that sanctuary. Things are out of order, and John doesn't seem to care. For example, in the opening verses of chapter 11, John records, "A certain man, Lazarus, was ill. He was from Bethany, the village of Mary and her sister Martha. (This was the Mary who anointed the Lord with fragrant oil and wiped his feet with her hair. Her brother Lazarus was ill.)" (vv. 1–2). The problem with this description is that Mary doesn't anoint Jesus' feet until the next chapter, John 12. John doesn't seem to care if things happen in order, and it's because he has a deep understanding of how God works.

God abides in an "eternal now." Everything that happens is the present from God's perspective. For us, the past is memory, and the future is only a dream. The only part of time that we consider to be real is the present; but really, the moment we are able to even recognize the present, it is already in the past. We never experience anything objectively. For instance, think about the fireworks you might see on New Year's Eve. From a distance you see the explosion of color in the dark evening sky, and then a beat later you hear the boom. You are actually hearing something that happened in the past—it just took time for the sound to travel from the fireworks through the air to your ear. The fact is, this is how we experience everything, not just fireworks. Everything we experience is on delay.

When you taste ice cream or pet your dog or hear an operatic aria, it takes time for your senses and nerves to tell your brain what you are experiencing. Most of the time this seems instantaneous. It seems that when you see the sun rise, that you're looking at the sun as it is, when in actuality it takes about eight minutes for the light to travel from the sun to Earth. So when you notice the beauty of the sunset, you are seeing the sun as it was eight minutes into the past. Or consider the stars shining in the night sky. The light we see from the stars has taken millions of years to get to the Earth from the far reaches of space, so when we look to the stars, we are seeing the stars as they were millions of years ago, through ancient light. When we look to the stars, light from millions of years ago is seen in the present.

God lives in an eternal now—a present moment that lasts forever. The past, present, and future as we know them don't make sense from God's perspective. From a heavenly perspective, everything is happening now. Think of the Doctor traveling in the TARDIS, his time machine. In the TARDIS, he can go anywhere in time and space, traversing millions of light years in a moment. This gives him a different perspective than we have—for the Doctor, talking to Shakespeare and seeing the end of the universe can happen at the same time. In a way, it's all "now" from the Doctor's perspective. In the episode "Smith and Jones," the first episode in season three, the Doctor walks up on an unsuspecting Martha Jones, takes off his tie, hands it to her then walks away without her ever knowing who he was or what he did. At the end of the episode, after the Doctor and Martha have worked together to save the world (of course), he tells her that he is a time traveler. She doesn't believe him, so he steps into the TARDIS and disappears. Moments later when the TARDIS returns, he is no longer wearing a tie. She remembers that he handed her his tie earlier in the day, so she stands there stunned saying, "But that was this morning." He responds, "Like I said . . . time traveler."[8]

The present is the only moment of time we consider to be real, yet it is so fleeting that it is nearly impossible to comprehend, and it is certainly impossible to contain or dissect. That's the place where God lives. That is where God's kingdom resides. Jesus said that God's kingdom is at hand, and it always is. That's the mystery! God's name means "I am," because God simply is. God wasn't, nor will God be. God always is. The good news is that Scripture says that we are God's children now, which is another way of saying that we are God's children always—"Dear friends, now we are God's children, and it hasn't yet appeared what we will be. We know that when he appears we will be like him because we'll see him as he is" (1 John 3:2).

"Now" is the most important time to God. What are you doing "now" to share God's love?

Like the church who didn't fix their out-of-order windows, what are your constant reminders of Christ's presence?

If heaven is an experience of an "eternal now," how does that change the way you live your life today?

Chapter Three

THE SONIC SCREWDRIVER IS MIGHTIER THAN THE SWORD

"Lord, the demons still are thriving in the gray cells of the mind; . . . speak your word that when we hear it, all our demons shall depart."[1]

What is a superhero without a villain? In large part, it is the Joker who makes Batman virtuous. Harry Potter is just some kid with a wand without a Dark Lord lurking about. Not long ago one of my daughters was singing Ursula's song, "Poor Unfortunate Souls," from the *The Little Mermaid* over and over again while we were in Disney World. I finally asked her why she was singing Ursula's song rather than Ariel's—after all, Ariel is the main character and she's the one who ends up being a princess. My daughter simply replied, "Because Ursula's more interesting." She's probably right.

Doctor Who has some great villains. (Though some are a bit cheesy, I will admit. You can't win them all). The baddies of *Doctor Who* aren't important because of how they try to destroy the universe time and time again, but why they do it. Daleks, Cybermen, the Master, The Silence, Weeping Angels, and many more all try to thwart the Doctor's plans in very particular ways. The Daleks think that the universe would be better off if they were the only species that existed. The Cybermen's mission is to "upgrade" all species so that all life forms are as efficient as a well-oiled machine. The Silence use amnesia as their greatest defense, but don't we all have things in our life we would rather forget? The interesting part is that all of these villains think that they are doing the right thing. From their perspective, it is the Doctor who is causing harm.

I assume that no one wakes up in the morning intending to do harm or purposefully wants to be destructive. The problem is that sometimes our definition of *good* really misses the mark. That's the problem with sin. Paul says in Romans 7, "The desire to do good is inside of me, but I can't do it. I don't do the good that I want to do, but I do the evil that I don't want to do. But if I do the very thing that I don't want to do, then I'm not the one doing it anymore. Instead, it is sin that lives in me that is doing it" (Romans 7:18b–20). In other words, sin makes us do what we don't want to do and unable to do what we want to do. It messes with our definition of what is good. Sin steals our potential for doing God's will, and makes us forget that God is always lovingly present.

Sin's ultimate goal is to make us angry with God's grace. In Luke 15, Jesus offers a parable about a man who had two sons. One son moved away and squandered everything while the other stayed behind and worked and earned his keep. When the younger son returns home, the father is overjoyed and graciously throws a party because he's so happy the son has returned. The older son becomes bitter and angry and jealous of the father's free grace toward his brother. When we become bitter and angry and jealous of God's grace, our sinful pride is winning. Just as the villains in *Doctor Who* always seem to have the upper hand, what the show teaches us is to never give up hope because the Doctor always seems to win. And the good news for us is that our battle is already won too—Jesus, the "healer of our every ill, light of each tomorrow,"[2] has already won the victory!

GOOD VERSUS EVIL

Good versus evil is a story almost as old as the story itself. Sometimes the battle between good and evil has definitive "good guys" and "bad guys," where the heroes and the villains are easy to distinguish. The good guy wears a sheriff's badge, the bad guy wears a dark trench coat; the good guy defeats the outlaw at high noon, and the town is safe once again.

Other times it might seem obvious who is good and who is evil, but the basic reasoning is somewhat the same, especially when each is living out his or her own definition of *good*. Batman fights to prove that there is such a thing as a universal moral code. The Joker creates chaos, not because he thinks he is doing evil, but because he thinks that "good versus evil" is a construct and doesn't really exist. To the American colonists, Samuel Adams was a freedom fighter. To the British, he was a rabble-rouser and troublemaker. The only difference is the context and one's definition of good.

The difference between good and evil becomes complex when we realize that the line between the two isn't out in the world where some people are completely good and others are purely evil. The line is drawn through each of us. Near the end of the Gospel of Matthew, Jesus tells his disciples a parable in which the Son of Man will separate the nations as a shepherd separates sheep from goats. The sheep, who have served their neighbor, enter into God's kingdom, and the goats, who have not, are thrown into the fire. The parable is told to communicate the importance of serving, but some take the parable too far and live as if there is a dividing line with some on the right and some on the left. When we draw a hard and fast line in the sand of who is "in" and who is "out," we typically draw it so that we are the sheep and those we disagree with are the goats. In truth, the dividing line runs right through our own soul.

EXTERMINATE! AND DELETE!

The woman saw that the tree was beautiful with delicious food and that the tree would provide wisdom, so she took some of its fruit and ate it, and also gave some to her husband, who was with her, and he ate it. – Genesis 3:6

Teenagers hold a special place in my heart. Being in high school is tough. I remember early in my freshman year it was difficult just trying to figure out where I was supposed to sit in the cafeteria. I didn't fit in with the athletes, that much was certain. So, do I brave trying to sit with the popular kids? Maybe the nerds and geeks have a spot open? What if all the tables are full?

Not knowing where one belongs makes someone a prime target for some of *Doctor Who's* greatest villains. The Daleks would invite you to join their table, but they would extract everything within you that wasn't anger or hate, and you would be encased in an art-deco tank made for protection. You would be indoctrinated in the destruction of any race that wasn't Dalek and given a voice modulator so you could scream "Exterminate!" with chilling effectiveness. Should the Cybermen find you, you would be "upgraded" into a robotic suit, making you incapable of feeling any kind of emotion and brainwashing you into believing that the destruction of all other races was simply a means to the end of a well-oiled machine. They would certainly offer you a place to fit in, but in the process you would lose yourself for all of the wrong reasons.[3]

Although their philosophies and motives differ, the Daleks and the Cybermen share a desire to be the only race in the universe, and there are no winners with this strategy. In a much less destructive, end-of-the-world way, this reminds me of a church who had a long-standing debate of whether to place the American flag or the Christian flag to the right of the pastor. One church member claimed the American flag needed prominence; another member claimed that using the Christian flag was more appropriate for the sanctuary. The problem is that both flags claim an authority to be in the prominent position to the right of the speaker. The pastor was asked to make a decision about which flag should be displayed, which is a lose-lose opportunity any way you slice it. It may be a bit tongue-in-cheek, but the pastor proclaimed that whoever was the first to arrive for worship on Sundays would have his blessing to put the flags where he saw fit. Some Sundays the American flag was to the right of the pastor. Other Sundays the Christian flag was displayed near the pulpit. I'm not sure this was the best solution, but the pastor's compromise completely diffused the heated debated, and now the changing flags are part of what make this church its own.

In a way, this is what the Doctor does in a no-win situation. As late-night television host Craig Ferguson surmised, the Doctor is about "intellect and romance over brute force and cynicism."[4] The Daleks are the most storied of the Doctor's villains. First appearing onscreen as nothing more than a plunger held mostly off camera in December 1963, the Daleks play a major role in making the Doctor who he is. As the story goes, Davros, an evil genius with a desire for genetic manipulation, created the Daleks as a means of winning a thousand-year-old war between the Kaleds and the Thals. As you might imagine, the Daleks he created are so ruthless and void of conscience that they destroy both races and even try to kill Davros himself. The Daleks never question authority, are virtually indestructible, and are so perverted that hate is their measure of beauty.

I find the Daleks intriguing not because they keep appearing, season after season, bent on destroying the universe, but because they are a great example of the problem of sin. I always get an eyebrow raise when I say from the pulpit, "sin is half right." I say this because sin is a perversion of God's first commandment of "Be fruitful and multiply" (Genesis 1:28 NRSV). Sin is like a cancer in the sense that it is great at multiplying; but it is never fruitful, meaning that sin performs half of God's commandment quite well. That's why sin is so tempting. It's so close to being right, but it never will be.

The Daleks think they are doing good—by their own perverse way of thinking, the universe would be absolutely better if they alone were in control. Likewise, the problem with sin is that it redefines the good. In Genesis 3 the serpent questions Eve, asking what God specifically said about the tree of the knowledge of good and evil. After the serpent says she will not die after eating the fruit, the woman sees that "the tree was beautiful with delicious food and that the tree would provide wisdom, so she took some of its fruit and ate it, and also gave some to her husband, who was with her, and he ate it" (Genesis 3:6). What's so wrong with wanting good food or seeking delight or being filled with a desire for wisdom? Nothing, except that the desire for what was good and delightful was now placed on the tree instead of its Creator. This was the first act of idolatry.

God put on flesh in the person of Jesus and was crucified on a tree so that our knowledge of evil might be transformed into a desire for good. A Dalek thinks it is doing good—the problem is that its definition of good is misguided. The Cybermen are a bit different in their approach to conquering the universe. The Daleks are fueled by hate, but the Cybermen run on apathy. Whereas the Daleks are a cautionary tale of genetic manipulation, the Cybermen reveal the horror of self-aware technology reminiscent of *2001: A Space Odyssey's* HAL or *The Terminator*.

HELPFUL TO A FAULT

The Sonic Screwdriver can do just about anything—except open doors made of wood, oddly enough.

In *Doctor Who* mythology, the Cybermen originated on Earth's sister planet, Mondas. After a global catastrophe that knocked Mondas out of orbit, the Mondasians became weak and frail. They began supplementing their failing bodies with inorganic machinery until they became more machine than animal. In order to complete the process of protecting their species, they eradicated all emotion, a perceived weakness. Unlike the Daleks' perversion of good, the Cybermen represent the false hope of perfection. They continuously upgrade in order to become faster, smarter, and stronger; but with each upgrade they increasingly lose the ability to love or share compassion or joy.

One day a certain ruler asked Jesus, "What must I do to obtain eternal life?" Jesus answered, "You know the commandments." The man said, "I've kept all of these things since I was a boy." Jesus replied, "There's one more thing. Sell everything you own and distribute the money to the poor. Then you will have treasure in heaven. And come, follow me" (Luke 18:18–22). When the man heard this, he went away sad because he was quite wealthy. Some would say that the solution would be for the man to sell his possessions and follow Jesus, but the Cybermen would say that it is the man's sadness that must be crucified.

Both the Daleks and the Cybermen multiply at alarming rates, but their venture is hardly fruitful. God commanded humanity to be fruitful and multiply, but sin entered and distorted the message. The problem with sin is that it is half right—it's great at multiplying, but it is never fruitful.

Which table did you sit at in the high school cafeteria? Were you able to find a place to belong?

Imagine a world in which everyone was like you. What would that look like?

Have you ever experienced how sin can distort the truth? How did God use that experience to show you what his truth looks like?

THE MASTER OF REJECTION

Jonah thought this was utterly wrong, and he became angry.... I know that you are a merciful and compassionate God, very patient, full of faithful love, and willing not to destroy. – Jonah 4:1–2

In *Doctor Who*, not all Time Lords are as heroic as the Doctor. In many ways, the Master is the Doctor's opposite. The Joker to the Doctor's Batman, the Master is a lunatic who uses deception and charm to control and enslave. Over the course of the show, we realize that the Master wasn't always crazy. In fact, he and the Doctor were children together on their home planet of Gallifrey; and as a rite of passage, all Time Lord children entering school were forced to look into the Untempered Schism, a tear in the fabric of space and time. Like the Doctor, some stare into the schism and become inspired. Others, like the Master, are driven to madness. The Master is a tragic figure. He is just as brilliant and talented as the Doctor, but his jealousy of the Doctor, coupled with his own narcissism and madness, make him the perfect nemesis.

Fundamentally, what separates the Doctor from the Master is the Doctor's ability to offer grace and the Master's inability to accept it. The rejection of grace is one of the oldest stories in the Bible. In Genesis 6–9, God looks at the world and sorrowfully sees that the world is full of wickedness and evil, so he decides it's time for a redo. God calls Noah and his family to build an ark and fill it with one male and one female of every living thing. Then it rains and pours for forty long days. Finally the rain stops, the waters recede, and Noah's ark lands on dry land on the top of Mount Ararat (or round-about there). Noah steps off the ark, builds an altar, and prepares a sacrifice for God. It is at this moment when there is seemingly a dramatic change in the nature of God. God says that never again will he destroy every living creature because of humanity's wickedness. From this moment on, God will not destroy evil—he will redeem it.

In that brief holy moment outside of the ark, God vows to never again destroy the world. God makes a covenant with Noah, sealing his promise, and places a rainbow in the sky as a reminder of his ever-lasting covenant. God repeats his vow over and over again, almost as if he is actively trying to stay his own hand. The bow in the clouds represents an archer's bow, meaning that if God ever decides to deal with sin in a grand way, he will be the one to take the death arrow—and this is exactly what God does by sending Jesus as a sacrifice for our sin.

Fundamentally, the story of the Flood is about God actively teaching humanity an important, life-giving lesson—how to forgive. After the man and the woman ate the forbidden fruit in Genesis 3, God called out to them asking, "Did you eat from the tree, which I commanded you not to eat?" (Genesis 3:11). It wasn't that God didn't know already know what they'd done—he was calling out to them, giving them an opportunity to confess so that they could receive pardon and forgiveness. Yet the only response is blame—the man blamed the woman, the woman blamed the snake, and the snake remained silent.

This passage is a story about human disobedience to be sure, but the story is foolish if the moral is, "Don't disobey, 'cause God's gonna thump you." Instead, the heart of Genesis 3–5 is a story of humanity's failure in accepting God's offering of confession and pardon. It is no mystery why the story of Noah and the Flood immediately follows Adam and Eve's failed acceptance of forgiveness. It is because the Flood story is fundamentally a story about God modeling what it means to confess and what it means to be forgiven. The story begins with God saying, "I'm sorry" (confession), and ends in Genesis 9 with God repeating the covenant promise (forgiveness) over and over again, like a parent teaching a child. Notice how the language in verse 16 changes, as if Noah is repeating the covenant back to God:

Verse 12: God said, "This is the sign of the covenant that I make between **me** and you and every living creature that is with you, for all future generations:

Verse 13: "I have set my bow in the cloud, and it shall be a sign of the covenant between **me** and the earth.

Verses 14–15: "When I bring clouds over the earth and the bow is seen in the clouds, I will remember **my** covenant that is between **me** and you and every living creature of all flesh. And the waters shall never again become a flood to destroy all flesh.

Verse 16: "When the bow is in the clouds, I will see it and remember the everlasting covenant between **God** and every living creature of all flesh that is on the earth."

Verse 17: God said to Noah, "This is the sign of the covenant that I have established between **me** and all flesh that is on the earth." (ESV, emphasis mine)

When Adam and Eve disobeyed, God desperately offered forgiveness, yet their self-preservation rejected his grace through blame-filled words. So God looked upon humanity and said, "Repeat after me…I'm sorry." God's confessionary tears fell from the sky, swelling the earth with a mournful lament. When the crying stopped, God knelt down with Noah and said, "Repeat after me…I forgive you."

During the final three episodes of season three, it looks as if the Master has finally taken over the earth. He creates a "Paradox Machine," which has enslaved humanity and allows him to start a new empire. In short, the Doctor, with the help of his companion, Martha, thwarts the Master's plan in a scene overflowing with Resurrection symbolism. As the Doctor moves toward him, the Master cries out, "It's not fair!" As the Doctor cradles his defeated and broken friend, he replies, "You know what I'm going to say. I forgive you."[5]

Sometimes it is difficult to forgive someone who has wronged you. But holding on to anger and resentment becomes a poison you drink to forget the pain. Peter asks Jesus a question that often rolls through my mind—"How many times should I forgive?" (Matthew 18:21). As difficult as it is to forgive someone, sometimes it is even more difficult to accept forgiveness when you are the person in the wrong. When we sin against our sisters and brothers, sometimes we feel like we deserve some kind of pain or punishment in return for forgiveness. But remember that after the Flood, God pointed the bow at himself as a sign representing that the next time God would deal with sin, he would be the one taking the arrow on behalf of humanity. And he did. He sent Jesus to earth to take on the sin of the world so that we might be eternally forgiven. God took the arrow—the nails and a crown of thorns and a cross—so that our sin will never again keep us from the heart of God.

What does God teach us about forgiveness through the story of the Flood?

Can you think of a time when someone offered you grace, but you felt you deserved punishment? Were you able to accept that forgiveness?

THE TOUGH PILL OF GRACE

"Look, I've served you all these years, and I never disobeyed your instruction. Yet you've never given me as much as a young goat so I could celebrate with my friends. But when this son of yours returned, after gobbling up your estate on prostitutes, you slaughtered the fattened calf for him." Then his father said, "Son, you are always with me, and every-thing I have is yours. But we had to celebrate and be glad because this brother of yours was dead and is alive. He was lost and is found." – Luke 15:29–32

Grace seems to be God's greatest gift when it is offered to us, but it can be a tough pill to swallow when it is offered to someone we think doesn't deserve it. One of the interesting things about the Doctor is that he rarely rolls into a situation with the intention of squashing a villain. David Tennant's incarnation of the Tenth Doctor was especially gracious—he often approached the baddies with eyes of compassion, assuming that their love of destruction is the result of a broken spirit. Rather than squashing evil at first blush, he offers first to help heal the hurt, and he almost always offers a second chance.

In the episode "Forest of the Dead," the Vashta Nerada, a microscopic cannibalistic swarm of creatures resembling a shadow, has been slowly killing an exploration team on a planet called "the Library." Near the end of the episode, the Vashta Nerada finally have the Doctor cornered. As the shadow approaches, he says to them, "You just killed someone I like. That is not a safe place to stand. I'm the Doctor, and you're in the biggest library in the universe. Look me up."[6] After a tense, momentary pause, the shadows retreat.

The Master is disgusted by the Doctor's grace toward his enemies, a command that is extensively explored in the Bible. In what is best known as the Parable of the Prodigal Son (or should it be called the Parable of the Angry Brother?), Jesus tells of a young man who asks for his inheritance early, the equivalent of saying, "Drop dead, old man" to his father. But his father honors his request and the young man leaves home, having the time of his life until he blows all of his money and finds himself sleeping with pigs because he has nowhere else to go. (Have you ever found yourself in a similar, rock-bottom place?) At some point, he realizes his foolishness and decides he has nothing to lose by going home.

POP CULTURE CROSSOVER

Twenty-nine actors have appeared in both *Doctor Who* and the Harry Potter film series. Among them, David Tennant, the Tenth Doctor, played villainous Barty Crouch Jr. in *Harry Potter and the Goblet of Fire*. Others include Michael Gambon (Professor Dumbledore), Imelda Staunton (Professor Umbridge), and John Cleese (Nearly Headless Nick).

The young man walks home, rehearsing his apology, but while he is still "far off" (aren't we all?) his father sees him and humbly and scandalously runs to meet him, interrupting the son's apology with extravagant grace. This would have been a fine ending to the story, except that it's not over. The older brother, who has been the "good" son, working in the fields this entire time, becomes furious. He says to his father,

> "Look, I've served you all these years, and I never disobeyed your instruction. Yet you've never given me as much as a young goat so I could celebrate with my friends. But when this son of yours returned, after gobbling up your estate on prostitutes, you slaughtered the fattened calf for him." (Luke 15:29–30)

The father's grace offered to the younger brother angers the older brother, and it is difficult to blame him. Certainly the older brother should have rejoiced to see his younger brother return, but his father's extravagant, almost reward-like response, leaves him exasperated. Grace is a tough pill for him to swallow.

Likewise, the Gospel of Matthew records a parable about a landowner who goes out to hire workers for his field. He hires people throughout the day for a single-day's wage. At the end of the day, the landowner pays the laborers, giving even those who had worked the fewest hours a full day's wage. When those who had been in the field all day receive the same payment, they become angry saying, "These who were hired last worked one hour, and they received the same pay as we did even though we had to work the whole day in the hot sun" (Matthew 20:12). The landowner simply replies, "Don't I have the right to do what I want with what belongs to me? Or are you resentful because I am generous?" (Matthew 20:15).

The older brother and those workers were angry not with what they had, but what was offered to those who they thought deserved less. This lesson rings as true today as it was when it was written. Whether it is in economics or politics or education or positions on the church council, we seem fine with what God has offered us as long as someone less deserving doesn't have more.

The Master sees the Doctor's grace as wasteful and weak. In his mind, he thinks of how much good the Doctor could do if he would just crush his evil enemies. This struggle plays out at the end of season eight in the episode "Death in Heaven." The Master gifts the Doctor with an unlimited army of Cybermen to try and prove that they aren't so different from one another—that given an army at his disposal, the Doctor could become a ruthless leader. Refusing the Master's gift, the Doctor replies:

> Thank you! I am not a good man! I am not a bad man. I am not a hero. . . . Do you know what I am? I am an idiot, with a box and a screwdriver. Just passing through, helping out, learning. I don't need an army. I never have, because I've got them. Always them. Because love, it's not an emotion. Love is a promise.[7]

Grace is God's greatest gift when it's offered to you, and it can be the toughest pill in the world to swallow if it's offered to someone you don't think deserves it. "Those who are last will be first" (Matthew 20:16) is a difficult truth if you find yourself at the front of the line. My son "was lost and is found" (Luke 15:24) is tough to hear if you're the older brother. He will "leave the other ninety-nine in the pasture and search for the lost one" (Luke 15:4) sounds extravagantly wasteful if you are one of the ninety-nine. Truth is no one deserves grace—not the last or the first or the lost or the found—that's why it's such an amazing gift.

Have you ever felt like the older brother in Jesus' parable? Why?

Have you ever felt like the younger brother in Jesus' parable? Why?

Do you have experience being both?

THE SILENCE OF A WEEPING ANGEL

But I will remember the LORD's deeds;
yes, I will remember your wondrous acts from times long
past. – Psalm 77:11

Jesus shows his crucifixion wounds to his disciple Thomas, and Thomas replies, "My Lord and my God!" (John 20:28). The next few sentences say, "Then Jesus did many other miraculous signs in his disciple's presence, signs that aren't recorded in this scroll. But these things are written so that you will believe that Jesus is the Christ, God's Son, and that believing, you will have life in his name" (John 20:30–31).

It's a fitting end to John's Gospel. Jesus is triumphant, the disciples believe, but don't close the book yet—John 21 begins by saying, "Later, Jesus himself appeared again to his disciples." You mean, there's more? Of course there is! Even though the Gospel ends in triumph and great belief, the reader is left asking, "What am I to do?"

Our Christian journey doesn't end with faith—it begins with God's grace and love for us. God first loved us in offering himself on earth in the person of Jesus so that we might know that life becomes an amazing blessing when we learn to serve one another, lift up the lowly, treat our bodies as sacred, and welcome the outsider. By following Christ's example, Christ begins to dwell within us, to abide in us. (See John 15:4.) Confession is only the beginning of the journey. Our story doesn't end with confession, and neither does John's. There is so much more!

John 21 begs us to remember the story, and to put it into action. Remembering the goodness is key, and this is why The Silence and the Weeping Angels are so dangerous—they are the bad guys in *Doctor Who* who don't simply kill you, but instead forever change who you are. Daleks change your DNA, removing everything but hate. The Cybermen "upgrade" you by erasing all emotion and placing whatever is left in a metal shell. Whether through genetic manipulation or emotion inhibitors, you are no longer the same after the Daleks or Cybermen find you. Much like the Daleks and the Cybermen are two sides of the same evil coin, the villains known as The Silence and the Weeping Angels destroy who you are in similar ways.

The Silence, first appearing in season five, are members of a religious order who vow to protect the universe from the Doctor, whom they consider a threat. Their weapon of choice is telepathic amnesia—in short, they make you forget. The more The Silence attack, the less of "you" you become. When you see The Silence, don't turn to run away, because the moment you turn, you forget that they were ever there. The Silence don't take your life—instead they effectively steal your identity by taking your memories.

The Weeping Angels prey on their victims in a different way. Believed to be ancient beings, the Weeping Angels have evolved to be the perfect assassins. When someone or something looks at them, they freeze and literally turn to stone so that they can't be killed. They appear to be stone angels or religious statues covering their eyes in mourning, but actually they cover their faces so that they will never see each other and freeze into stone indefinitely. Like The Silence, the Weeping Angels don't kill their victims; rather they feast off one's potential energy. According to *Doctor Who*, each of us produces a kind of potential energy in time—that is, our accomplishments, our emotions, our dreams, and so on, create a kind of energy. If a Weeping Angel catches you, it sends you back in time and feasts off of your potential energy that remains into the future. So, in short, The Silence and the Weeping Angels are bad guys. The Silence cause you to forget the world; the Weeping Angels cause the world to forget you.

After the Resurrection, Simon Peter seems to forget that Jesus is alive. He encourages the disciples to go fishing—in essence saying, "Okay, boys, time to go back to your day job." The disciples go out fishing, and they catch nothing. Just after daybreak, they see a man standing on the beach, but they don't recognize the man as Jesus. He calls out to them, "Children, have you caught anything to eat? . . . Cast your net on the right side of the boat and you will find some" (John 21:5, 6). So they cast their nets on the other side of the boat, and they catch more fish than they know what to do with. "Then the disciple whom Jesus loved said to Peter, 'It's the Lord!'" Peter puts on some clothes and jumps in the water (v. 7). What an odd detail to mention—that Simon Peter puts on some clothes before going to Jesus. It is odd to mention, unless you remember a story from way back—God gives Adam and Eve everything they need, but they disobey him. Their first act following their disobedience was to try and clothe themselves to hide their nakedness because they were ashamed. (See Genesis 3.) Peter, who had recently denied having even known Jesus, sees his Lord on the lakeshore and immediately clothes himself. Then he jumps into the water to swim to Jesus. He doesn't wait for the boat to come in with the fish—he jumps into the water, fully submerging himself. *Remember the story.* Earlier in the Gospel, Peter asks Jesus, "What are you doing? Why are you washing my feet?" Jesus replies, "Unless I wash you, you won't have a place with me" (John 13:8). Peter, with his denial fresh in his mind, dunks his whole body in the water, hoping to wash away his clothed shame.

CREATING A LEGEND

Verity Lambert, the first producer of *Doctor Who* from 1963 to 1965, was also the first female producer ever hired by the BBC. She was responsible for casting William Hartnell as the First Doctor, setting the tone for the entire series.

Jesus sat on the shore cooking breakfast, preparing fish and bread. *Remember the story.* Jesus multiplied the fish and the loaves, and through the abundance of God there were twelve baskets left over (see John 6). The fish Jesus was preparing did not come from their catch. It was already there. That is so true of God's grace, which goes before us—a meal had already been set for them, and they were simply asked to eat and be filled. When they had finished breakfast, Jesus asked Simon Peter, "Simon son of John, do you love me more than these?" (John 21:15). *Remember the story.* When Jesus first met Simon he named him Peter. He seems to have lost that title, at least, for now. When Jesus says, "Do you love me more than these," we're not sure what "these" are. I imagine that Jesus might be pointing to the burning charcoals. The last time Peter was around charcoal is when he was warming himself in the courtyard while he was denying Christ. *"Do you love me more than these? Do you love me more than power or preservation or status? Do you remember these burning coals? The coals with which I used to burn Isaiah's lips to make them clean?[8] The coals I now show to you so that you might be clean?"* "You know I love you," Peter replies. Jesus answers, "Feed my sheep" (John 21:17).

Jesus tells Peter to "feed my sheep" once for each time that Peter denied Jesus. I wonder what the world would be like if we answered our doubts and our denials with good works. It is easy to respond with good works when we are faithful and times are good. I wonder what it would be like if when we are faced with doubt or anger or frustration that we respond with good works anyway. *Remember the story.* Lord, you know I love you, but I'm just so angry…*go and feed my sheep.* Lord, you know I love you, but I'm doubting…*go and feed my sheep.* Lord, you know I love you, but that guy who claims to be a Christian…*go and feed my sheep.*

Often we too easily forget the good news of what Christ has done. Sin prompts us to forget that we are connected to one another, that we are the sheep called to feed each other. We turn away from a brother or sister in need, and soon we forget that they were ever there. This is precisely what The Silence and the Weeping Angels try to steal—your ability to remember God's goodness and that, through Christ and the Holy Spirit, we have the potential to change the world. *Remember the story.*

> *Have you ever felt Jesus asking, "Do you love me more than these?" What tends to come between you and your devotion to Jesus?*
>
> *What are some ways that help you "remember the story"?*

THE REDEMPTION OF EVIL

God didn't send his Son into the world to judge the world,
but that the world might be saved through him.
— John 3:17

The baddies of *Doctor Who* are in the business of causing harm, but what exactly is the Doctor supposed to do with them? If he goes out to rid the universe of the entire race of Daleks, he would become the enemy he despises. The hallmark of a great superhero story is the tension between the hero and the villain, especially when the line between the two is blurred. If Batman ever kills the Joker, the Joker wins. If Superman kills Lex Luthor, then Superman has lost his moral ground. If Luke Skywalker gives into his anger and kills Darth Vader, then he will have turned to the Dark Side and all is lost. If Frodo Baggins keeps the ring of power...you get the idea.

So what are we supposed to "do" with evil? First we have to understand what evil is. There are three ways in which we might understand the existence of evil. First, evil is the result of sin—the separation between humanity and God. In the beginning, when God created the heavens and the earth, God prepared a place for humankind so that we could have a loving relationship with him. It wasn't long, though, before simply loving God was no longer enough. Even though God offered humanity 99 percent of all of the trees in the garden, we wanted 100 percent. We saw that the tree of the knowledge of good and evil was good for food, pretty to look at, and would make one wise. The problem is that we saw that the *tree* was good rather than the *Creator* of the tree. God and humanity became separated, and this separation is sin. Sin made it difficult to follow God's first commandment: "Be fruitful and multiply" (Genesis 1:28 NRSV). As we discussed, in a way, sin is half right, which is why it is so tempting. Sin accomplishes only half of God's first commandment—it is great at multiplying, but it is never fruitful. So evil is the "fruitlessness" sin delivers. With the arrival of sin, our work became plentiful, but fruitless because it could not bring us a relationship with God.

A second way of understanding evil is that it is a spiritual force that stands opposed to God. Satan is usually the prime suspect when things go awry. In large part, Satan is evil itself. I don't often preach on Satan because there is a temptation to make Satan sound more interesting than God—it seems that even mentioning Satan plants unhelpful seeds, but knowing Satan's beginning is helpful. Satan first appears in Scripture in 1 Chronicles 21—"Satan stood up against Israel and incited David to count the people of Israel" (v. 1 HCSB). Interestingly, 2 Samuel 24 is an earlier recording of this same story: "Again the anger of the LORD was kindled against Israel, and he incited David against them saying, 'Go, number [the people of] Israel and Judah'" (v. 1 ESV). In other words, the earlier story remembers that God's anger was kindled against Israel, but the later story attributes God's anger to Satan. There is no back-story or footnote or flashback to explain who this Satan character is. In other words, Satan's origin seems to be from an editor's pen.

There are several stories[9] within the Old Testament that include the Hebrew word, *ha-satan*, which can either be translated as "Satan," or simply, "accuser." Sometimes this adversary is human, someone who stands against another individual or group. Other times Satan is a spiritual figure, as in the story of Job. In the Book of Job, God and Satan, or the accuser (*ha-satan*), barter over Job's faithfulness. God allows the accuser to have all of Job's possessions, but the accuser is not allowed to harm Job himself. Later in the story, the accuser is given the opportunity to harm Job, but he is never given the right to kill him. Outside of Job, Satan is relatively missing from most of the Old Testament. In the Gospels, Satan, now called the devil, is spiritual force residing outside of the presence of God, having power and influence in the world in opposition to God's work. The devil appears to Jesus in the wilderness offering earthly power in exchange for Jesus' subjugation.[10] Unlike the seemingly irresistible influence of the devil in the Gospels, the later books of the New Testament suggest that the devil is a spiritual force that Christians are called to and are able to resist.[11] The Book of Revelation suggests that the devil brings about wrath upon the earth, devouring and conquering humanity to the point in which God must finally intervene. A great battle ensues, and the devil is eventually bound and thrown into eternal damnation.

Often *Doctor Who* plays with origin stories and how cultural narratives came to be. In "The Satan Pit"[12] the Doctor discovers the Sons of Light imprisoned an evil creature (red skin, horns, and all), which is the origin of all Satan-like figures in human history. This evil creature has the ability to influence people to perform acts of destruction and manipulation. The creature also tempts the Doctor in giving up his "faith"—his understanding of how the universe works. "The Satan Pit" seems to suggest that even though we might disagree on who or what Satan is, temptation and sin and evil permeate all cultures.

Another way to look at evil is to see it as "nothingness," a negation of good. Think of it like this. In mathematics there exists an expression {-2}. This {-2} does not exist in and of itself. It only exists in its relation to {0}. Evil is much like a negative number because evil is an expression of humankind's separation from God. Scripture teaches us that good can be a result of evil, or more appropriately, that God can bring about good in the midst of evil. For example, it is possible for a negative number to have an absolute value: $|-2| = 2$.

Absolute value is always a positive. No matter the negative number, it is possible for that negative number to have a positive absolute value.

I don't mean to suggest that you can attach a number to sin, or that if you sin four times, you can ask for forgiveness four times and then you're back to "zero." My point is that God provides absolute value, which is always positive. The cross—the crucifixion of Jesus, the single most sinful human act—has its absolute value in the Resurrection. So God doesn't destroy evil—instead God redeems it and transforms it. If God chose to deal with evil through destruction, I'm not sure any of us would still be here. In God's mercy, God redeems evil through Jesus Christ and the power of the Holy Spirit. This is what the cross is about!

The cross, a symbol of death, was transformed through Christ's resurrection to be a symbol of life. So what are we supposed to do with evil? If we too quickly jump to eradicate evil through force and power, we will quickly become that which we vow to destroy, like if the Doctor used the Master's army of Cybermen to eradicate his own enemies. Through love, compassion, justice, and mercy, Christ made sure that death no longer has the last word. Jesus said in Matthew 5 that we are to "turn the other cheek," to "let go of anger," to "love our enemies," and pray for those who persecute us. In other words, through Christ we have the power to resist sin so that the world might know that sacrificial love is in fact more powerful than evil.

In your own words, what is the difference between destroying evil and redeeming evil?

How does Jesus' sacrifice on the cross help us understand what to "do" with evil?

Chapter Four

BIGGER ON THE INSIDE

*The grace of the Lord Jesus Christ, the love of God, and
the fellowship of the Holy Spirit be with you all.*
— 2 Corinthians 13:13

One of Doctor Who's longest running gags is the phrase, "It's bigger on the inside," when someone steps into the TARDIS for the first time. Outside it looks like a simple British police box, but inside it's a whole other thing. The trick is that the inside of the TARDIS is in a different dimension from the outside. I'm not sure how it works—the show dismisses it as Time Lord architecture. It's difficult to imagine blueprints where one side of a door is in a different dimension from the other side, but explaining interdimensional drafts just might be easier than understanding or explaining the Trinity.

There are plenty of metaphors the church has used over the years to attempt to describe the Trinity: that it is like water because water can be in three forms at the same time; or the Trinity is like a star because there is the star, the heat from the star, and the light the star emits; or the Trinity is like a three-leaf clover with three distinct leaves of the same plant. But all of these metaphors fall apart on some level.

Trinity is a word the church uses for God. God is Father, Son, and Spirit all at the same time. Even though the word *Trinity* never appears in Scripture, God has revealed the divine nature in three distinct persons. The closest the church has come to really explaining this profound truth is the Athanasian Creed written sometime in the late fifth or early sixth century, which reads in part:

> We worship one God in Trinity, and Trinity in Unity; Neither confounding the Persons; nor dividing the Essence. For there is one Person of the Father; another of the Son; and another of the Holy Ghost. But the Godhead of the Father, of the Son, and of the Holy Ghost, is all one; the Glory equal, the Majesty coeternal. Such as the Father is; such is the Son; and such is the Holy Ghost. The Father uncreated; the Son uncreated; and the Holy Ghost uncreated. The Father unlimited; the Son unlimited; and the Holy Ghost unlimited. The Father eternal; the Son eternal; and the Holy Ghost eternal. And yet they are not three eternals; but one eternal. As also there are not three uncreated; nor three infinites, but one uncreated; and one infinite. . . .

As I said, it may, in fact, be easier to understand interdimensional architecture than to fully explain the Trinity. What we do know is this: the Trinity is a picture of how we understand who God is. It is what it "looks like" when God enters into our world. When the Doctor enters the scene, we see a blue box. When God enters our lives, we experience Father, Son, and Spirit. In other words, like the TARDIS is what it looks like for the Doctor to travel through time, the Trinity is what it looks like when God travels through time. If a picture is worth a thousand words, the Trinity must hold an infinite amount. I guess the Trinity must be bigger on the inside?

THE HEART OF THE TRINITY

Even though the word *Trinity* never appears in Scripture, almost all mainline Christian denominations profess that God is in three persons: Father, Son, and Holy Spirit. There are lots of different ways of talking about the mystery of the Trinity. As a writer, I find it helpful to think about the Trinity as "Idea, Action, and Interpretation." Every good story begins with an idea. What story needs to be told? What is the best way to tell it? Who needs to hear it? In a way, God the Father is like the idea—the origin and the inspiration. Jesus, the Son or Word of God, is like the action of writing down the idea. When you write, the idea becomes real and shareable. Sometimes the word on the page doesn't match the original idea, but Jesus is the perfect action of God's holy idea. In Christ, the words or action exactly match God's will. It's like when Jesus was praying in the garden before his arrest: "Father, if it's your will, take this cup of suffering away from me. However, not my will but your will must be done" (Luke 22:42).

God is like the idea. Jesus is like the idea being perfectly written. The Holy Spirit is like the interpretation of what's been written. If I say the word *read*, is this something you do in the present or something you do in the past? Whether you read "read" in the present or you've "read" in the past depends on interpretation and context. The idea can be perfect, and the words explaining the idea can be perfect, but without interpretation, neither the idea nor the word make any sense. The Holy Spirit is the author of interpretation. Scripture says the Spirit is our teacher and guide (John 15:26). This isn't the only way to understand the Trinity, of course. At some point, all of our metaphors break down, which is why it is all a matter of faith.

1+1+1=1

"Holy, holy, holy! Lord God Almighty!... God in three persons, blessed Trinity!"[1]

All superheroes have a super power. Some have super strength or great intelligence or an endless supply of bat-shaped gadgets. Time travel is the Doctor's super power. Actually, I guess you would say that the TARDIS is actually the Doctor's super power because the TARDIS allows the Doctor to travel anywhere in space and time. It looks like a blue British 1960s police box; it pops in and out of time; and it makes an incredible, iconic "whooping" sound when it appears. I don't pretend understand how this works. As a fan, you just have to accept that the TARDIS is what it is. Neither do I fully grasp the nature of the Trinity—how God the Father, Jesus the Son, and the Holy Spirit are three in one, and that, for us, God exists as the Creator, the Redeemer, and the Sustainer of Life.[2]

In the beginning, when God created the heavens and the earth, Scripture says the earth was a formless void and darkness covered the face of the deep, while a wind from God swept over the face of the waters. And God said, "Let there be light" (Genesis 1:3). Here, in the very beginning of our story, we have God, a wind (or spirit) of God, and the Word of God, all working together to bring about creation. Later in the story, it is interesting to see that when God creates humanity, God says, "Let us make humanity in our image" (1:26). Let *us*. In *our* image. It's plural—God, the Word of God, and the Spirit of God are in mutual relationship, bringing about humanity. From the beginning, God is understood as being plural.

97

Adding to the Lexicon

Doctor Who is responsible for several additions to the *Oxford English Dictionary*. *Dalek* and *TARDIS* have both been added because of the show's popularity.

How is it that God can be three and one at the same time? There's been lots of ink spilled on this question over the centuries, and none of the metaphors we can think up to explain the Trinity can fully do it justice, but there are a few helpful images we can consider. Some explain the Trinity by using the properties of water—water can be a solid, a liquid, and a gas, sometimes at the same time, but it's still just H_2O. Some explain it by looking at a triangle—a triangle has three points and three sides, but it's still the same shape. What I have found helpful is to think about my dad—my dad is my father, he is also my uncle's brother, and he is also my grandparents' son—all at the same time.

Confused yet? I don't blame you if you are. The church has been thinking about the Trinity for two thousand years, and the concept still makes our heads spin. It is difficult, maybe impossible, to understand the depth of the nature of God. But sometimes it helps to have a picture in our heads to explain an unexplainable concept, which is why thinking of a triangle or a three-leaf clover is helpful in picturing how the Trinity works. In the same way, the TARDIS gives us a picture of what it looks like for the Doctor to travel through the whole of time and space. In a similar way, the Trinity is what it looks like when God moves through time with us. God has chosen to reveal himself to us as Father, Son, and Spirit. Images help our minds grasp the unexplained, which is why it's helpful to see the Doctor step into a blue box so he can travel through time. It's why we sometimes draw a triangle, call it the Trinity, and move on.

But what do you suppose the Trinity really looks like? I think Saint Augustine really nailed it when he gave us the image that the Trinity is the Lover, the Beloved, and the love they share. John Wesley often talked about "means of grace"—that is, the ways we receive God's grace: through Bible study, prayer, worship, communion, baptism, and so on. The means of grace are outward and visible signs of an inward and spiritual grace.[3] In other words, when you feed the hungry, the outward and visible sign is the food you are sharing; the inward, spiritual grace is your heart undergoing a transformation as you break bread with someone. It's like a wedding ring (outward and visible sign) as a symbol of a deep and abiding love two people share (inward, spiritual grace). When we gather for worship, when we sing songs and give gifts and pray and listen to the Word of God, these are outward and visible signs of an inward spiritual grace.

These outward and visible signs represent what's happening in the life of God. You see, the Trinity is God and Christ connected in love. So when the church worships, the church as the body of Christ and God are connected in mutual and shared love. In other words, the Trinity looks like worship. The Trinity looks like the person on your left singing praises full of joy. The Trinity looks like the person on your right who can't lift her eyes to the altar because of a great sadness. The Trinity looks like the sinner finally exhaling because he has been forgiven. The Trinity looks like the elderly man who can no longer stand during songs and the child who dances with reckless abandon in the aisles. When we gather together for worship, we see the Trinity right before our eyes in a very real way.

Worship brings us where we need to be just like the TARDIS brings the Doctor where he needs to be. In the Gospel of Mark, Scripture says that after Jesus' baptism the Holy Spirit forced Jesus into the wilderness (Mark 1:12). It doesn't say that the Spirit invited Jesus into the desert, or that the Spirit politely suggested that Jesus go. It says that the Spirit forced him to a barren place. The TARDIS doesn't always take the Doctor where he wants to go. In fact, it often doesn't. He sets a course to see the beauty of a crystal rain in a far-off world, and the TARDIS takes him to a war-torn earth in need of healing. Sometimes worship isn't all we wish it was. Maybe the sermon is lacking or the songs are too slow. Maybe that guy you can't stand sits in your pew or the girl who has to know everything about everyone spots you at the welcome desk. Sometimes worship is less than the holy practice it should be, but if we are open to the Holy Spirit, worship will always bring us where we need to be.

The Trinity is bigger than we could ever understand, but what we can know is that God's love for us will never be exhausted and that God calls us to actively participate in sharing his love for the world. Because when God moves through our space and time, we call it love.

In your own words, how you would describe the Trinity? Why does it matter that God is in "three persons"?

How does your community of faith talk about the Father, the Son, and the Holy Spirit?

BIGGER ON THE INSIDE

God is love. – 1 John 4:8

It happens almost every time someone new walks into the TARDIS—"It's bigger on the inside!" they say with amazement. The small, blue, 1960s-era British police box looks so unassuming from the outside, and that's kind of the point. The TARDIS, an acronym for "Time and Relative Dimension in Space," is the Doctor's time traveling spaceship, originally meant to blend in with its surroundings—wherever it ends up—so as to not draw any attention to itself. Unfortunately, somewhere along the way the chameleon circuit became damaged beyond repair, leaving it stuck in its iconic police box form. (I'm sure having the same prop is also helpful when working on a shoestring production budget!)

DRIVING INSTRUCTIONS

According to Professor River Song, the iconic whirring sound the TARDIS makes is because the Doctor drives it with the parking break on. Engineers created the sound by scraping keys across the bass strings of a piano, and then playing the recording backward.

One of the most extraordinary things about the TARDIS, apart from the ability to travel through all of time and space, is that it is bigger on the inside than it is on the outside. The interior of the TARDIS exists in a different dimension than the exterior. One way to think about it is to think about the TARDIS as your smart phone. The phone itself can fit into a breadbox, but once connected to the Internet, there is a seemingly infinite amount of information lying behind the finger-sensitive glass screen. The three-dimensional phone is the window into a two-dimensional world of zeros and ones. The TARDIS is a four-dimensional vehicle with a three-dimensional world on either side of its doors. So, yeah—it's bigger on the inside.

This "bigger on the inside than outside" idea is a beautiful metaphor when we think about the Trinity, which is a confusing concept for many of us. God, three in one? It is rumored that Saint Augustine said that the Trinity is best understood as: the Lover, the Beloved, and the love that they share, meaning the Trinity is God and Christ, connected in shared and mutual love. This love between God and Jesus, or the Father and the Son, is bigger on the inside than it is on the outside. Think of it this way. In 1929, Rene Magritte painted the famous "The Treachery of Images."[4] The painting frames a simple brown pipe with a French caption that reads, *"Ceci n'est pas une pipe,"* or "This is not a pipe," though there is most certainly a pipe on the canvas. So, which is it? The painting is not a pipe; rather it is a picture of a pipe. The Trinity is simply a picture of who God is and how the church has discerned God's actions in the world. The Trinity doesn't reveal everything there is to know about God, but it does reveal what God has to do with us.

Let's take a look at another piece of art. During the fifteenth century, Russian painter Andrei Rublev[5] created an icon depicting the three visitors Abraham entertained in Genesis 18. Rublev used the story of the three visitors to create a worshipful artwork revealing the nature of the Trinity. The icon presents three figures sitting around a table. All three of the figures have the same face, representing that the three persons of the Trinity—Father, Son, and Spirit—are all one and the same. The person at the center of the table and the person on the right are both looking toward the person on the left who is looking back at the other two. This represents that the Son and the Spirit look to the Father as the Father looks to them. Again, the heart of the Trinity is mutual and shared love. The hands of each figure also reveal the different roles of the persons of the Trinity. The Father has relaxed hands of peace, the Son's hands are blessing the cup sitting in the middle of the table, and the Spirit's hands are pointing toward the earth—the place where the Spirit is working today. Finally, behind each figure represents the place where the persons of the Trinity are revealed. Behind the Father there is a house; the Son—a tree; and the Spirit—a mountain.

The icon's color palette reveals the Trinity's beauty. All three figures are wearing blue. Blue represents the color of divinity, the color not bound by time or space (ahem, also the color of the TARDIS). The figure in the middle is wearing dark brown/red with blue, representing Jesus' full humanity and full divinity. The figure on the right, representing the Holy Spirit, is wearing green with blue, signifying divinity and spiritual growth.

But the most surprising thing about Rublev's icon painting is that there is actually a fourth person in the picture—you! This represents how God invites us into his own heart, giving us a place at the table. God invites us to actively participate in what he is doing in the world. God did not become human in the person of Jesus just so that Jesus would die for us on the cross. Jesus also lived! Jesus fed the hungry so that we might share God's abundance with the hungry. Jesus welcomed the outcast so that we would open our doors to those whom society sees as unlovable. Jesus healed the sick so that we might humbly care for those in need. The Trinity is a picture of who God is—the Lover, the Beloved, and the love they share. The awesome thing is that when we share love with each other through kindness, generosity, and service, we share the very essence of God.

Scripture tells us, "God is love" (1 John 4:8), and it is a love that will never, ever be exhausted. God's abundant love is a gift that keeps on giving. When we learn to love our neighbor and love our enemies, we fall even deeper in love with Christ and become more and more satisfied by being in this presence. It is the cup that "spills over" (Psalm 23:5). God's love both satisfies and leaves us desiring more... because it's bigger on the inside.

What picture of the Trinity makes the most sense to you?

What does it mean to you that Scripture says, "God is love"?

Is there anything else that you might describe as being "bigger on the inside"?

ALWAYS ALONE BUT NEVER ALONE

Go, report to John what you have seen and heard.
– Luke 7:22

The Doctor is a lonely traveler. In fact, for hundreds of years he thought he was the only survivor of the great Time War. It must be a solemn thought to realize you are literally one of a kind. When the Doctor travels alone, he becomes angry, bitter, and vengeful, so as often as he can he travels with what he calls a "companion." Of course, his companion is usually a beautiful young woman, but that's beside the point, I guess. The Doctor is always looking for a partner to share in his adventures. He typically meets someone he finds interesting, charmingly opens the doors to the bigger-on-the-inside TARDIS, promises a trip to anywhere in time and space, and asks where he or she would like to go.

Even though time travel sounds amazing, traveling with the Doctor is dangerous, difficult, and often asks you to surrender everything. One day Jesus was walking along the shore of the Sea of Galilee when he called out to some fishermen to follow him. Scripture says they dropped their day jobs and followed (Mark 1:16–20). Goodness, it sounds so easy, doesn't it? I want to warn you—I am about to say a dirty word. There's no way around it. It's a word you do not use in polite conversation. You don't bring it up amongst strangers. You cringe when you see it on a book cover. Are you ready for it? *Evangelism.* There, I said it.

What images come to mind when you read that word? When I was in college, *evangelism* conjured images for me of a street preacher, a man carrying a sign rivaled in size only by his Bible, screaming at the top of his lungs of how I was going to hell. Do you think of the same image? Some use John the Baptist as the model for their fiery, in-your-face way of communicating the gospel—"You children of snakes! Who warned you to escape from the angry judgment that is coming soon?...The ax is already at the root of the trees. Therefore, every tree that doesn't produce good fruit will be chopped down and tossed into the fire" (Luke 3:7, 9).

Indeed, hearing the gospel is a powerful force that can wake us up and drive us into deep questions and demanding places, but that's also only half of the story. In the Bible, it's interesting to see how John's fiery fervor ceases when he meets Jesus face-to-face. Once he sees Jesus his ministry changes. Instead of talking about axes ready to chop down barren trees, he looks to Jesus and says, "Look! The Lamb of God" (John 1:29). Later in Jesus' ministry, John's disciples ask Jesus if he is The One. Jesus says, "Go, report to John what you have seen and heard. *Those who were blind are able to see.* Those who were crippled now walk. People with skin diseases are cleansed. *Those who were deaf now hear. Those who were dead are raised up. And good news is preached to the poor.* Happy is anyone who doesn't stumble along the way because of me" (Luke 7:22–23, emphasis mine). Apparently Jesus wasn't nearly as angry as John—and many others—expected the Savior to be. Jesus doesn't yell or chastise or dish out guilt as he walks the shoreline of the Sea of Galilee. He calls out to the fishermen and says, "Follow me, and I will make you fishers of people." In other words, he is meeting them where they are for who they are, speaking to them in a language they can understand.

Many years ago, after graduating college with a degree in music, I began to think about entering into ministry. After visiting several seminaries, one in particular really felt like home to me—Duke University. While visiting the campus, I decided to go into the chapel at Duke and pray about whether God was calling me to become a Blue Devil. I sat in silence for about twenty minutes or so, then I prayed, "Lord, I know I'm not supposed to ask this, but can you let me know if this is the right place for me? A sign would be helpful." At that moment, the organ started playing! It felt like God was speaking to me in the language the Lord knew I could understand. The affirmation was mind-blowing. Little did I know that the organ professor played in the chapel every day at 12:15 p.m. sharp, but to me it felt like a miracle.

Jesus called the men to put down their nets and follow him. They didn't have to stop fishing, he said, but the kind of fishing he was calling them to would now be done for the glory of God. Jesus called not only fishermen, but tax collectors and zealots and even a man who would eventually betray him. The Doctor opens the TARDIS doors to regular people. One of his companions, Donna Noble, seems as ordinary as you and me. She was a temporary worker living with her parents, with few aspirations or dreams. The Doctor invites her to travel with him, and in time they both discover that she happens to be the most important person in the universe. Donna's story is a reminder about how precious each of us is. In God's eyes, we are important and valuable and loved. So what if you never climb Mount Everest or have a big house or invent a new kind of peanut? What if you're "just" a teacher or an accountant or a stay-at-home mom? Perfect! Christ invites you to follow him and truly live.

But what about those who don't get out of the boat and follow? After calling Peter and Andrew, Jesus goes to the second boat, where James, John, and their father Zebedee are. He calls out to them, and

James and John leave their boat and their father and follow Jesus. Jesus called out to five people that day, and only four dropped their nets. What about Zebedee? Is he rejecting Christ by staying in the boat? It's not even clear that Jesus called for Zebedee to follow; the story simply says, "He called them. They followed him, leaving their father Zebedee in the boat." What do we with Zebedee? What do we do when our coworker refuses our invitation to come to church? What if your spouse stays home while you and the kids go to church?

It seems to me that, for some, following Christ means they will drop their nets—whether the net is a career or addiction or something from the past that needs redeeming. For others, being a disciple means to go—to pick up the net, to try something new, to go to new places and follow God's leading along the way. And still others may hear, "Keep up the fishing, friend, and tell everyone what you saw today."

Some of the Doctor's companions go with him on the TARDIS to far-off worlds to fight monsters and to revel in the wonders of the universe. Others stay on earth to do the difficult work of staying behind. When we choose to follow Jesus, he promises to be with us every step of the way, no matter where we are and what we are doing. He promises to show us the way to life. Could it be that all five who heard Christ that day on the water became disciples? Drop your net and follow. Pick up your net and follow. Keep on fishing and follow. Join with me in the work of the Kingdom.

In what ways does your community of faith share the gospel message?

How did you first get connected with your faith community?

Do you find yourself dropping your net or fishing in the boat for the cause?

SUNFLOWERS

"The way I see it, every life is a pile of good things and bad things.... And we definitely added to his pile of good things."[6] – the Doctor, to Amy Pond

Most of the time *Doctor Who* is simply a fun show to watch—the Doctor and his companion discover that someone or something is trying to take over the universe; it seems that all hope is lost, but by the end of the hour, the Doctor has won and goodness has prevailed. Sometimes the episodes stretch our imagination on the nature of time, or challenge how we understand identity or goodness. Every now and again, an episode is profoundly meaningful, expressing the beauty of what it means to love and to fight for what's right. And then you come across the episode, "Vincent and the Doctor," and you're left speechless.

In this episode, the Doctor and Amy Pond are looking at art in the British National Gallery when they notice that something in one of Vincent van Gogh's famous paintings seems off. They travel back in time and discover that Vincent is battling demons, both real and imagined. The real, but invisible, alien monster haunting Vincent leaves him in psychotic fits of sadness and rage, so the Doctor moves in to defeat the beast and save the day. But with the real monster gone, the Doctor quickly realizes Vincent's biggest foe is actually the monster of depression. Unappreciated and sometimes reviled in his hometown, Vincent fears that his work and his life are meaningless, so the Doctor and Amy take Vincent back to the present-day British National Gallery so that he can see how important his life's work will one day become. In one of the most beautiful scenes in *Doctor Who* history, Vincent stands off to the side while he overhears the museum curator tell a group of visitors that Vincent wasn't just one of the most important artists in the world, but that he was one of the greatest men who ever lived.

Amy and the Doctor take a joyful and smiling Vincent home, where he says goodbye to them in grateful tears and with a new perspective on his work and life. Happily, Amy and the Doctor head back to the gallery, excited to see how Vincent's paintings might have changed after their visit. His famous paintings still remain, but Amy is devastated to discover that Vincent still committed suicide in a fit of depression. She feels that nothing they did for Vincent actually mattered, but the Doctor holds Amy close and says:

> The way I see it, every life is a pile of good things and bad things. The good things don't always soften the bad things, but vice versa, the bad things don't necessarily spoil the good things or make them unimportant. And we definitely added to his pile of good things.[7]

The camera zooms in, and we see that Vincent's famous painting, "Sunflowers," now says "For Amy."

DOCTORS THROUGH TIME

Though the Doctor is now well over 1,200 years old on the show, the actors who have played him have a wide age range—so far the oldest actors have been 55, and the youngest, 27.

Depression isn't sadness—it's a "nothingness," a deficit of feeling. I tell my church members how it is important to cry, to lament, and to be angry at injustice and pain—it's when we lose the ability to offer tears that we really need help. The Book of Job is a masterpiece, offering a blueprint for what we are called to do in the midst of depression and hopelessness. As the story goes, Job loses his possessions, his family, his health, and then eventually slips into depression, shaking his fist at God asking "Why?" At first, his friends Eliphaz, Bildad, and Zophar get it right—they simply sit in silence with a suffering Job. But they eventually break the silence with unhelpful advice and hollow words. Then "out of the whirlwind" (what a truthful and breathtaking image), the Lord answers Job, saying,

> "Prepare yourself like a man;
>> I will interrogate you, and you will respond to me.
> Where were you
>> when I laid earth's foundations?...
> In your lifetime have you commanded the morning?...
> Can you issue an order to the clouds?"
>> (Job 38:3–4, 12, 34)

Job withdraws his "why" question, but God continues,

> "Do you have an arm like God....
> Look at Behemoth, whom I made along with you....
> Can you draw out Leviathan?" (Job 40:9, 15; 41:1)

God's actions sound harsh until you realize just what God is doing—God is taking Job on a tour of the universe. God is offering Job the most beautiful sights any single human has ever seen. It's like flying to the future on a TARDIS and discovering, like Vincent, that your life matters. God surrounds Job with as much beauty as he can muster. What a beautiful picture of what we can do for someone who is in the grip of depression—surround the person with beauty.

Several years ago I joined a team that was providing hurricane relief in New Orleans after Katrina. We were charged with gutting out Ms. Helena's home, which suffered an eight-foot storm surge and a three-week drowning in four feet of stagnant water. We pulled out dry wall and baseboards, moved pictures and books to the curb, and cleaned mold from essential structural beams. Near the end of our week, I had the chance to visit with Ms. Helena on her front porch. As we sat together, I asked her how she was feeling. She broke an awkward silence with, "Thank God for the flood."

"Excuse me?" I said.

"Do you see that oak tree in my yard?" she said. "If it hadn't been for the flood, the wind would have thrown the tree into my house, destroying it beyond repair. So, I thank God for the flood."

It was a humbling conversation. How was it that, in the midst of such suffering, she was able to thank God for anything? We had just thrown away almost everything she owned, and yet she was hopeful. Paul writes in Romans,

> "We even take pride in our problems, because we know that trouble produces endurance, endurance produces character, and character produces hope. This hope doesn't put us to shame, because the love of God has been poured out in our hearts through the Holy Spirit, who has been given to us." (Romans 5:3–5)

It sounds like an empty promise of sorts, and it is if we don't read Paul's words carefully. Paul does not say that suffering produces hope, but that we move from suffering to hope as a process.

Suffering is devastating because being in the midst of suffering seemingly erases possibility. It is difficult to see past your own face when you are suffering, because it seems like suffering will never end, that there won't be a tomorrow. This is why being in a place of hope is so important. Hope is the embodiment of possibility. Hope does not disappoint us, as Paul says, because "hope" is possibility. Suffering looks at a blank page and sees nothing. Hope looks at the same blank page and sees endless possibilities.

Suffering produces endurance, and endurance produces character, and character produces hope, and hope does not disappoint us. In other words, we suffer because we love. We look at the brokenness of the world, and our heart breaks over what breaks God's heart. This is why Christ suffered on the cross. Jesus looked over Jerusalem and wept. He suffered on the cross, taking on the sins of the world so that the world might be saved. He suffered and endured the cross, showing us the Christian character of love so that we might experience the hope of resurrection. It's like hearing Ms. Helena say, "Thank God for the flood." It's like Amy seeing her name on Vincent's work, knowing that even though a life was cut short, it was a life that mattered. The cross is the beauty of God because it is the only thing that offers us enduring hope.

Have you, or someone you know, experienced suffering? Where did it lead you?

Why do you suppose in this episode of Doctor Who *that Vincent van Gogh decided to dedicate "Sunflowers" to Amy instead of another painting? What's the significance of sunflowers?*

Have you ever had a "Thank God for the flood" moment?

FISH FINGERS AND CUSTARD, IN REMEMBRANCE OF ME

Do this in remembrance of me. – Luke 22:19

"Some days, everybody lives,"[8] Professor River Song says at the end of the two-part story "Silence in the Library/Forest of the Dead." That's the Christian hope, isn't it—to really live? The Gospel of John reminds us,

> What came into being through the Word was life,
> and the life was the light for all people.
> The light shines in the darkness,
> and the darkness doesn't extinguish the light.
> (John 1:3b–5)

Christ came so that we might find life, to live in a light more powerful than the darkness we know too well.

When Jesus gathered with his disciples on the night before his crucifixion, he broke bread and poured out wine and said, "Do this in remembrance of me" (Luke 22:19). Let's take a moment to unpack just what Jesus is offering here. First, we must "do." Christianity is not a passive life. Living in Christ is an "on the move" kind of life. It is fighting the good fight of justice. It is working to end oppression and hate and fear. It is giving up your life to bring about a world that doesn't spin because of money or power or might, but thrives on love, selflessness, honesty, and hope.

"Do this," Jesus says. What is the "this"? "This" is the beautiful and difficult work of reconciliation. On Jesus' last night, he gathered with Matthew the tax collector, who was working for the government, and Simon the Zealot, who was trying to overthrow the government. What brought these two men together? Christ did. It wasn't their politics. It wasn't their economic status or income level. They came together because they could both see that Christ is what it means to live. Jesus was there with Matthew the "yes man," Simon the rebel, Thomas the doubter, the hot heads James and John, Peter the denier, and Judas the betrayer. How could you get all of these broken people in the same place for the same purpose? By offering Christ. By breaking bread. By welcoming people. By offering purpose. "Do this," Jesus said.

"Do this in remembrance of me." We gather at the Lord's Table in remembrance of Christ, which is an action of both the head and the heart. Remembering is more than recalling. Yes, we recall how Jesus lived, died, and lived again; but remembering is the act of recalling and making it part of who you are. The head recalls and the heart affirms experience and claims it. Our identity is rooted in our memories, so when Jesus asks us to perpetually remember him, Christ is offering his story to be our story. In other words, we are to "remember" Christ, to literally re-member to bring Christ back into our lives each and every day. We remember Christ, inviting Christ to dwell within us, as we pray in hope, "Christ, remember us when you come into your kingdom." And of course, this remembering happens in community, an open community. The table is set for all. You have done nothing to earn a seat at the table. All that is asked is that you receive and keep receiving so that you may be transformed, so that your life begins to resemble this table.

One of the most rewarding things about being a parent is seeing your children begin to do good things without being asked. My daughter Isabelle now brushes her teeth and gets dressed by herself and picks up her toys—well, her favorite toys—by herself. She doesn't do these things to please herself, necessarily—these actions are simply now part of her habits and who she is. "Do this in remembrance of me," Jesus commands. The table is set for you, and you are asked to receive the grace of Christ so that your life begins to resemble Jesus' life and worship becomes a habit. As we begin to share goodness and mercy and love with our neighbor, when we begin to fall deeply in love with God, we begin to realize, as Paul says—"I no longer live, but Christ lives in me" (Galatians 2:20).

Holy Communion is like our own little time machine, so to speak. When we commune together, we commune with all of the saints, with everyone who is in Christ. Bread and wine, by the power of the Holy Spirit, is a receiving of the heavenly banquet. Christ invites us to be his companions—literally "one with whom we break bread." If there is a center of the universe, it is here because, at the table, time is indeed "wibbly-wobbly." At the table we receive Christ, the light of the world, the eternal boundary of the universe. At the table we discover what it means to live and live abundantly. At the table we receive the presence of Christ, the Great Physician, so to speak; and as River Song said, "Some days, when the Doctor comes to call...everyone lives."[9]

How does your community of faith celebrate Holy Communion?

Traditionally Jesus has sometimes been called "The Great Physician." What name for Jesus makes the most sense to you?

Who is the Doctor to you?

NOTES

CHAPTER 1: THE OLDEST QUESTION IN THE UNIVERSE

1. "Asylum of the Daleks," *Doctor Who* (series 7, episode 1), British Broadcasting Corporation One (London: BBC, September 1, 2012).

2. "Last of the Time Lords," *Doctor Who* (series 3, episode 13), British Broadcasting Corporation One (London: BBC, June 30, 2007).

3. Stanley Hauerwas, *Matthew* (Grand Rapids, MI: Brazos Press, 2007), 35.

4. "Human Nature/Family of Blood," *Doctor Who* (series 3, episodes 8 and 9), British Broadcasting Corporation One (London: BBC, May 26, 2007 and June 2, 2007, respectively).

5. "The Doctor the Ultimate Hero—Steven Moffatt on the Eleventh Hour Panel—Doctor Who," accessed March 25, 2015, https://www.youtube.com/watch?v=LWHWQJFSQjo.

6. I should at least mention Richard Hurndall and his work playing the First Doctor in "The Five Doctors" (which originally aired November 23, 1983) after the death of the original First Doctor, William Hartnell.

7. Before I get any angry e-mails, between the Eighth and Ninth incarnations there was the "War Doctor," played by John Hurt. So, numbering the different Doctors gets a bit wonky at this point.

8. See also Galatians 6:15 and Ephesians 2:15.

9. "The Big Bang," *Doctor Who* (series 5, episode 13), British Broadcasting Corporation One (London: BBC, June 26, 2010).

10. Let's throw in a few more questions: Does River Song really know the Doctor's name? Is River Song really the Doctor's wife?

11. "The Wedding of River Song," *Doctor Who* (series 6, episode 13), British Broadcasting Corporation One (London: BBC, October 1, 2011).

12. "The Day of the Doctor," *Doctor Who* (specials 2013), British Broadcasting Corporation One (London: BBC, November 23, 2013).

CHAPTER 2: GOD AND TIME AND GOD'S TIME

1. "Silence in the Library/Forest of the Dead," *Doctor Who* (series 4, episodes 9 and 10), British Broadcasting Corporation One (London: BBC, May 31, 2008 and June 7, 2008, respectively).

2. "Day of the Moon," *Doctor Who* (series 6, episode 2), British Broadcasting Corporation One (London: BBC, April 30, 2011).

3. "Blink," *Doctor Who* (series 3, episode 10), British Broadcasting Corporation One (London: BBC, June 9, 2007).

4. Matthew 17:1–9; Mark 9:2–8; Luke 9:28–36.

5. "Blink."

6. Ibid.

7. "The Girl Who Waited," *Doctor Who* (series 6, episode 10), British Broadcasting Corporation One (London: BBC, September 10, 2011).

8. "Smith and Jones," *Doctor Who* (series 3, episode 1), British Broadcasting Corporation One (London: BBC, July 6, 2007).

CHAPTER 3: THE SONIC SCREWDRIVER IS MIGHTIER THAN THE SWORD

1. Thomas H. Troeger (lyrics) and Carol Doran (music), "Silence, Frenzied, Unclean Spirit," *The United Methodist Hymnal* (Nashville: The United Methodist Publishing House, 1989), 264 stanzas 2, 3.

2. Marty Haugen, "Healer of Our Every Ill," *The Faith We Sing* (Nashville: Abingdon Press, 2000), 2213.

3. For a great miscellany on all things *Doctor Who*, check out *Whoology* by Cavan Scott and Mark Wright (London: BBC Books, 2013).

4. "*Doctor Who*—Lost Opener from Craig Ferguson—*The Late Late Show*. With Lyrics," accessed April 12, 2015, https://www.youtube.com/watch?v=0sK5d3oshp8.

5. "Last of the Time Lords," *Doctor Who* (series 3, episode 13), British Broadcasting Corporation One (London: BBC, June 30, 2007).

6. "Forest of the Dead," *Doctor Who* (series 4, episode 9), British Broadcasting Corporation One (London: BBC, June 7, 2008).

7. "Death in Heaven," *Doctor Who* (series 8, episode 12), British Broadcasting Corporation One (London: BBC, November 8, 2014).

8. Isaiah 6:7.

9. See Numbers 22, 1 Kings 11, 1 Kings 22, Job 2, and Zechariah 3.

10. See Matthew 4, Mark 1, Luke 4.

11. See Ephesians 6:11 and James 4:7.
12. "The Satan Pit," *Doctor Who* (series 2, episode 9), British Broadcasting Corporation One (London: BBC, June 10, 2006).

CHAPTER 4: BIGGER ON THE INSIDE

1. Reginald Heber, "Holy, Holy, Holy! Lord God Almighty!" (1826). Public domain.
2. See Genesis 2:7, Job 27:3, and Romans 8:10 as examples of the Spirit as Sustainer of Life.
3. The Catechism of *The Book of Common Prayer* of the Episcopal Church, pp. 845–862.
4. "The Treachery of Images" (1929) by Rene Magritte, http://www.renemagritte.org/the-treachery-of-images.jsp.
5. *Wikipedia*, s.v. "Trinity (Andrei Rublev)," accessed April 13, 2015, http://en.wikipedia.org/wiki/Trinity_(Andrei_Rublev).
6. "Vincent and The Doctor," *Doctor Who* (series 5, episode 10), British Broadcasting Corporation One (London: BBC, June 5, 2010).
7. Ibid.
8. "Forest of the Dead," *Doctor Who* (series 4, episode 9), British Broadcasting Corporation One (London: BBC, June 7, 2008).
9. Ibid.

ACKNOWLEDGMENTS

I am so thankful to share this study with you, but this study would not have happened without some very special people. I first have to thank my wife, Christie, and my lovely daughters Isabelle, Annaleigh, and Cecilia for sharing me with the ministry in general and this study in particular. I have to especially thank my dad, Rick. He started me on *Doctor Who* at a very early age. He also asked me the difficult questions of faith that shaped and formed my experience of God. He's my hero. My mother has also been my biggest fan. I literally wouldn't be here if it weren't for her.

I must also lift up my colleagues in ministry and the churches I have served. Thank you to Reverend Ken Irby, who first gave me the green light to host a *Doctor Who* sermon series. Thanks to Reverend Dr. Sam Wells for showing me how to overaccept God's gifts. Thanks to Reverend Mark Goins, who helped make all of this possible! I am grateful for Angie Cason, whose talent is beyond my imagination. Thank you to Dr. Andy Crome for hosting "Doctor Who and Religion" day at the University of Manchester, and to

Elizabeth Coody for letting me know about said event. I must also acknowledge the support of my colleagues in the Louisiana Conference of The United Methodist Church and the grace I have received from the churches I have served.

I am so thankful to Abingdon Press for offering me this opportunity. To the team: Susan Salley, Ron Kidd, Alan Vermilye, Tim Cobb, Marcia Myatt, Tracey Craddock, Camilla Myers, Sally Sharpe, Sonia Worsham, and Nancy Provost. I also must lift up Lori Jones for making me sound better than I deserve—you have a gift, my friend.